В. Габрина

ZOO BABIES

by Vera Chaplina

Zoo Babies

by
Vera Chaplina

ISBN: 1-58963-576-0

Fredonia Books
Amsterdam, The Netherlands
http://www.fredoniabooks.com

CONTENTS

OUR ZOO

(By Way of a Preface)

I HAVE LOVED animals all my life, and ever since I can remember I have kept all sorts of fledglings, puppies and other young animals.

It was nice to be welcomed home by baby crows with wide-open beaks, and I liked it when baby sparrows did not fly away from my extended hand, and baby rabbits jumped boldly into my lap.

At the age of fourteen I joined the young biologists' circle in the Moscow Zoo. Our instructor was Pyotr Alexandrovich Manteifel, a well-known biologist and a true lover of nature. He taught us to love animals and study nature.

Our circle was very small and friendly. The attendants we helped by cleaning the cages and feeding the animals, and the research workers by our observations, and by noting in our diaries the behaviour of the animals, weighing them and registering their growth. And in a short time I began to work at the Zoo myself.

In those days the Moscow Zoo was nothing like what it is now. The animal houses were cramped and inconvenient. Many of the cages were empty, for there were very few animals and birds at that time.

But by the end of 1924, the Zoo had begun to fill up. Animals arrived in great consignments from all over the world. Soon there was no room for them and new enclosures and cages were made wherever possible, and the old ones enlarged and improved.

The New Territory of the Zoo was then being laid out. It was new in every way. Big enclosures with artificial hills were made for the mountain goats, spacious runs for the beasts of prey, with a deep moat instead of bars. At the back of the run were cages built in a big artificial cliff.

All this grew up under our very eyes. We were familiar with every stone, and we all tried to use our spare time for the good of the Zoo.

Of course, we could not take part in the actual building, but we did quite a lot in helping to plant the ground with trees and bushes.

The first thing seen by visitors now entering the New Territory of the Moscow Zoo is a small swamp. This was once a grassy hollow, with a few bushes scattered over it. We were asked to turn it into a swamp. To make a swamp! This sounds very strange. We are accustomed to the idea that thousands of acres of swamp are being drained in the U.S.S.R., and now we were to *make* a swamp—and in Moscow! But we did not find it at all strange.

And so, equipped with sacks, spades and buckets, we set off for the Tsaritsin ponds (not far from Moscow). There, very carefully so as not to damage the roots, we dug up small mounds overgrown with reeds and willow herb, wrapped them in damp sacking, loaded them on our lorry, and took them back to the Zoo.

Each member of our circle had a separate plot assigned for transplanting this green stuff. We had to get our mounds firmly established in the future swamp. This was very difficult, much more difficult than transplanting the most delicate flowers.

We placed them carefully on artificial risings, faced them with turf, and watered them several times a day. It was hard work. But how delighted we were when all the plants took root and the hollow filled with water! It began to look like a real swamp, and long-legged herons, rosy-breasted flamingoes, and many other water-birds were transferred to what was now perhaps the prettiest nook in the whole Zoo.

When the New Territory was ready it was gradually filled with all sorts of animals. To the Goats' Mount came yaks and mountain goats, to the Polar World—polar bears and polar foxes, and to the Animal Islet—tigers, bears, wolves and other beasts of prey.

At first the beasts of prey were kept in cages in the middle of the islet, opening into spacious runs. But before admitting the public to the New Territory we had to let the animals out of their cages to make certain they could not jump across the moat. This had to be done in the early morning while the town was still asleep.

Very few of the Zoo employees went home the evening before the animals were to be let out. I myself did go home, but I kept worrying about oversleeping, and went back at three in the morning. Early as it was, everyone was there.

The first to be let out were the tigers. The five huge striped cats took a few cautious steps and settled on their haunches. They had never tasted liberty. Born in captivity, they had spent their lives on the wooden floor of a cage, and the sensation of earth beneath their paws was unfamiliar to them. These great, powerful beasts trembled with fear like helpless kittens. But gradually the strangeness wore off and they began looking for a way out, getting up on their hind legs, sniffing at the walls, and trying to jump across the moat. But this they could not do. They fell into the water, snorted, and hurried back to dry land—it was not only the width of the moat, but the coldness of the water which alarmed them. Leaving people on duty beside the tigers, we went to release the panthers.

There were two of them. They had both quite recently arrived from Central Asia. They had been caught in traps, and one of them was lame. It was extremely difficult to make them leave their cage. They huddled in a corner and refused to come out.

At last one was driven out with the utmost difficulty.

When it found itself in an open space its muscles went taut. At the sight of the people around, it spat and crouched low, and then all of a sudden ran lightly up the sheer face of the cliff, as if it were on the paths of its familiar mountain-side. It all happened so swiftly that no one could prevent the animal from alighting with a second bound higher up on the cliff, where it disappeared through a top window in the Animal Islet. In a few minutes the shutters on all the windows were closed to prevent further escape.

The panther was only caught the next day. After this escapade it was put back in its cage, and wolves were let into the run.

At last all was in readiness. Cages, pens and runs were filled with animals. The paths of the New Territory were sprinkled with fresh sand. Proud and happy, we opened wide the gates of the New Territory, and welcomed in our first visitors.

And so the New Territory of the Zoo was opened to the public, and a new stage of our work began.

There had always been a great deal of experimental work done at the Zoo, observations made, diet and treatment studied. Young animals in the Moscow Zoo receive every care. They are weighed and measured just as babies are at children's consultation centres. But it is much easier to handle children than baby animals. The great thing is to know what sort of a mother the baby animal has. If she is tame, well and good—if she is savage, beware!

It is sometimes very difficult to take a baby animal from its mother. The mother has to be transferred to another cage and one must wash one's hands and wipe them on the litter on the floor of the sleep-ing-place before picking up the little one, otherwise, sensing an un-familiar smell on her babies, the mother may kill them or refuse to feed them.

We young biologists were very keen on our work. We spent whole days, and very often nights, in the Zoo. Some were interested in birds, others in insects or fishes, but I liked baby animals most of all. It was my dream to bring up animals which I could approach, touch and fondle without fear of being bitten.

In the spring, numbers of baby animals were sent to the Zoo from all over the Soviet Union. And there were always baby animals in the Zoo whose mothers would not feed them. These had to be fed by hand. Many of them were of great interest and value.

In 1933 I was entrusted with the care of all motherless youngsters.

My task was very difficult. There were books showing how to bring up calves, but nowhere could I find a book telling me how to bring up a baby lynx or a hyena whelp. I had to find out everything for myself, and not seldom to learn by my errors.

The baby animals were scattered all over the Zoo, and my helpers and I spent a lot of time running about. Then I decided to organize a special enclosure for baby animals. It was my aim to bring them up not only strong and healthy, but in such a way that animals of different species should live peacefully side by side.

I gave much thought to the best way to arrange the enclosure. This is how we did it: we placed separate cages for the various animals around a spacious run, where they were all let out together. Each animal had its own toys and games.

There was a pool in it for the animals to bathe in hot weather. In a word it was a regular kindergarten for baby animals, with its own time-table for hours of play, rest, and meals.

TELLING THE TIME WITHOUT A CLOCK

The baby animals knew when feeding-time came round just as well as the grown-up animals did. When the hour approached they stopped playing as if at a signal, and waited in great excitement for their food, their heads turned towards the kitchen.

The kitchen door creaked. The first to respond to this sound were the dingoes, the foxes and the wolves. They would run up to the gate and wait there. After them hastened the lions, the bears and the rest.

They were fed in their cages. There was never any need to drive them in. They knew their cages well and the moment the doors were opened, went in of their own accord. Mistakes were seldom made, and then only by the fox cubs, who always tried to snatch more than their share, and got into the neighbouring cages. If dinner happened to be delayed the animals were greatly disturbed.

ANIMAL RIOT

While the cubs were quite tiny they were fed every two hours. Then the intervals between meals were gradually lengthened. The babies did not at all approve of such changes, and each expressed displeasure in its own way. They were particularly upset on the first day of the change in their time-table. The lunch hour came round, and no food was brought to them. They kept glancing at the kitchen, but the door did not creak and nobody came out. The babies began to show signs of anxiety.

The dingoes tore up and down the enclosure. Every now and then they stood still, raised their heads, and whined. The whines grew into howls, and were taken up by the wolf cubs, who tried to get into their locked cage, gnawed at the bars, and flew into a passion. The bear babies stopped playing, squeezed themselves against the bars of their cage and moaned softly. If any of my helpers chanced to enter the enclosure at such a moment all the baby animals would flock to her, the bear cubs standing on their hind legs and roaring, the dingoes leaping, the wolf and fox cubs getting underfoot. The lion cubs, usually so self-controlled and calm, were just as bad.

They all begged for food and got so excited that they had to be put into their cages. Hardly were the doors of the cages opened, when the little things rushed into them, jostling one another in their haste. Once inside, they quieted down a little, but when they saw that no food was forthcoming, they again began throwing themselves about and making a noise. The bear cubs roared, the dingoes and wolf cubs howled, the lion cubs mewed plaintively. They raised a regular riot, and all because their usual meal-time had been changed. But in a few days they got used to the new time-table and order was restored.

TASTES DIFFER

The tastes of animals differ as much as their ways of eating. The baby jackals were fond of liver-and-lights. The lion cubs liked their meat fresh, and turned away from stale meat. The bear cubs, on the contrary, did not care for freshly killed meat and considered stale meat a dainty.

One day the fox cubs buried some meat in the ground. It lay there a long time and went bad. The cubs, released from their cages, dug it up. None of them would touch the meat, except the bears, but they fell upon it with zest. Each pulled it his own way. They had a real fight over it. We tried to entice them away with bread and even sweets—for they are sweet-tooths. But it was no good. The baby bears tore up the putrid meat and devoured it with grunts of pleasure.

So you see how tastes differ among animals!

Young animals eat grass, too. When fresh-mown grass was brought to them they all fell upon it, plunging into it, and throwing it about. They did not eat it just as it came, each one chose the parts he liked best. The bears were not very particular, they would snatch up tufts of grass, and munch it with smacking noises, like pigs. The dingoes, wolf cubs and lion cubs would pull out a stem at a time and chew at it for a long time, rather clumsily.

Visitors were astonished at this sight, and thought the cubs were not fed properly and ate grass from hunger. We had to explain that animals require vegetable nourishment, too. In a wild state they get it for themselves, but in the Zoo it had to be brought to them.

REST HOUR

After a meal the animals were supposed to rest, just like people in sanatoriums and rest-homes, and children in kindergarten. On Sundays and holidays, when there were always a great many people in the Zoo, the animals did not get their rest. They had to be pushed out of their cages by force after feeding-time on these days. Their movements were languid and slow, and they did not attempt to play, but just lay about. The wolf cubs, whose tummies get as round as a water-melon after eating, could hardly move, their eyes closed of themselves, and if they did start playing they sometimes brought up their food, and afterwards they were hungry. On ordinary days all animals are supposed to rest after food. For one or two hours the Zoo becomes a realm of sleep. After this the babies get up and beg to be let out to play.

They were up to all sorts of tricks when they were let out after their rest! The dingo puppies would immediately seize a broom, and chase one another, snatching it away, followed by all the rest. They would get hold of the broom, pulling it in all directions, and when one of them tore the broom from its handle, the chase would begin all over again.

ANIMAL FACES

Visitors were often surprised to see how easily we who worked in the young animals' enclosure knew them from one another.

But we knew our own animals, just as a countrywoman knows her own chickens from the neighbours'. For us each one looked different.

Each had its own face, character and habits. Look at the fox cub Liska, running by! You can recognize her immediately by her blunt, light-coloured muzzle and gentle eyes. You can pick her up, she won't bite. And there's her brother Lisok, with a dark muzzle and narrow angry eyes. Don't touch him—he bites! Frantik is a fox cub, too, but he isn't a bit like the other two, he's slim and long-legged, and has a sly face. And the dingoes and the wolf cubs are all different, too. Their very way of walking is different. Vulka is the strongest of all the wolf cubs. This can be sensed in his calm, confident gait. And his brother had to be removed from the enclosure. He used to attack the weaker animals, especially the kid, and he was treacherous, you couldn't trust him.

If we had not known all the animals apart, our work would have been impossible, we might have mixed them up and put an animal in the wrong group. Out-of-doors they play peacefully together, but inside the cage it is a different matter. The cage is their home. Any stranger venturing inside does so at his own risk.

The young animals lived in their enclosure till the autumn. By that time they had grown up; some were sent to menageries, the rest were transferred to ordinary cages, and the enclosure was shut up till the spring.

KINULI

MOTHERLESS

K INULI IS a lion cub. She was born in the Moscow Zoo. I called her Kinuli because her mother abandoned her.* Nobody knows what made the lioness refuse to feed her cubs. They crawled about the cage, squealing, and she passed by them as if she did not see them. On the second day of their lives three of the cubs died, but I took away the fourth, the very smallest, just in time to save its life.

The cub was quite cold and did not move. You might have thought it was dead, but for its feeble breathing. The first thing to do was to

* *Kinuli* means *abandoned.—Tr.*

get it warm as quickly as possible. But I did not know how and where this could be done. Then I remembered that there was an incubator in the ostrich house. I hurried over, made room in the incubator, spread a cloth on one of the shelves, and put the cub on it.

I did not go home at all that day, but stayed to look after the baby. I rang up home, so that they should not be worried and said: "Expect me tomorrow with a lion cub." My mother gasped, and one of the neighbours took the receiver out of her hand and raised such a hulla-baloo when she heard I intended to bring a lion home, that everyone came running up to see what was the matter. Then they began shout-ing all together that I ought to be turned out of the flat, that they would complain to the militia, and there was such a din and outcry that I stopped listening and hung up.

The next day I went home with my new baby.

It was raining, and very cold. I put the cub inside my coat to keep it warm, and got on to a tram. I don't know whether it was the motion of the tram, or whether the fur lining of my coat reminded the cub of its mother, but it suddenly began to fidget. I tried hard to quiet the baby by stroking it, but it was no good. It scratched me with its sharp claws in its efforts to get out, and suddenly gave a piercing mew, if the hoarse, long-drawn-out sound, like the creaking of a door, may be called mewing.

All heads were turned in my direction and all the passengers stared at me in astonishment. Not wishing to attract the conductor's attention, I hurried out on to the front of the tram. A man followed me there. He hemmed and hawed, and at last asked me what it was that had given such a strange cry from inside my coat. I showed him the cub and told him where it came from, asking him to say nothing about it, for fear I should be put off the tram. Apparently he did not keep his word, and before we reached Pushkin Square all the passengers

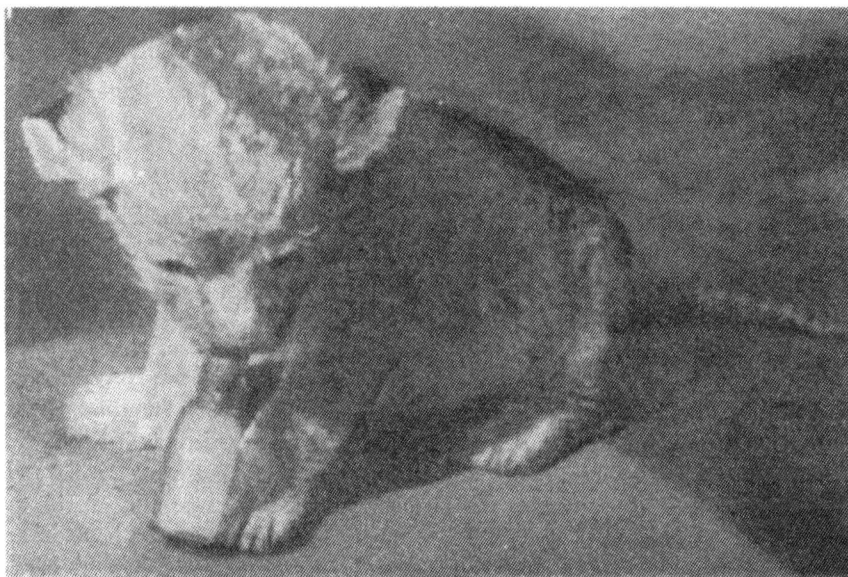

came to have a look. Everyone wanted to get a glimpse of the lion cub, and when I was getting off, the conductor leaned out and shouted after me:

"Why didn't you show *me* the lion cub?"

So I had to show it to him.

Before going home I went to a chemist's shop. I wanted a rubber nipple like the ones they feed babies with, only softer. I spent a long time looking for a suitable one. Some were too hard, some too big, some too small. The girl in the shop showed me one after another. But I simply couldn't find the right one. At last the girl lost patience and told me that since I couldn't choose a nipple the mother had better come herself. So I had to tell her that the mother was a lioness in a cage, and couldn't come, and that every minute wasted might cost the cub its life. And by way of proof I showed her the lion cub.

I never expected this would make such an impression on her. In another minute every nipple in the shop lay on the counter before me. No doubt the shop girl had never before catered for a baby animal.

By our combined efforts we chose a suitable nipple and I bore it off in triumph.

They were all expecting us at home, but I did not show the cub to anyone that day. I had to get a place ready for it, to warm it and feed it. I had no box that would do. While my son Tolya cleared the things out of a suitcase I ripped the fur lining from my coat. It was rather like the lioness's fur and Kinuli lay quietly in it. The bodies of new-born animals do not accumulate sufficient heat. We have all seen a dog tucking her puppies beneath her to warm them with the heat of her body. The lion cub had no mother, so I put a bottle of hot water under the fur and the cub lay in this nest as if it were beside its mother.

The news that a lion was living in my room spread rapidly over the whole house. Strangers came to our door, sometimes alone, sometimes in groups, apologizing for the intrusion and asking to be shown the lion. They came cautiously into the room, but when they saw the lion cub they were rather disappointed—it was not a bit like a grown-up lion. They inspected it long and earnestly, then thanked me, and went out as cautiously as they had come in. Before leaving they would advise me to be very careful, in case the lion ate me up when it grew bigger.

Everyone in the flat grew very fond of Kinuli, except Masha, my maid, who had taken a dislike to the cub from the first. She was opening the door to visitors all day long, and closing it after them, and she had to clean up the room, for Kinuli brought a lot of disorder into it. Our small room was turned into something between a nursery and a laboratory; everywhere were cotton wool, vaseline, boric acid, rubber nipples, syringes, in fact everything required for the bringing up of a baby—and the cub required a great deal.

I fed Kinuli every hour. As soon as she woke up I gave her a bottle of warm milk. It was a tiny bottle, containing not more than two tablespoons of milk, and I had to feed Kinuli very often, for she drank two pints of milk a day. To make it more like lion's milk I added diluted cream. The cub pawed the bottle contentedly and drank with loud sucking noises.

She required attention night and day.

When Kinuli slept, the whole flat was plunged in silence. Everyone went about on tiptoe and spoke in a whisper, and the children guarded the cub's slumbers just as well as the grown-ups did. The only one who did not care was Masha. She would bang the saucepans about on purpose and mutter: "Bringing all sorts of pests into the house." And the "pest" lay quietly in the suitcase, sucking her comforter. She sucked it so perseveringly, even in her sleep, that she rubbed her nose sore against the ring and the comforter had to be taken away. But Kinuli had got so used to it that she couldn't go to sleep at all, and kept nozzling about, with piteous cries.

The children saved the situation. Tolya, Lyona, Slavik, Galya and Yura took turns to sit up with Kinuli. To feed her and see that she did not cry they even drew up a list of those on duty. The children were very proud of the work entrusted to them, and boasted among their friends that they had a lion cub at home.

I now began to look about for a dog. It was hard for me to take care of Kinuli by myself, and a dog would be a help. After prolonged search I settled on Perry. Perry was a collie, and she lived in the Zoo. She had no puppies, but she was very kind-hearted and docile, she never touched the animals, and once even suckled a dingo.

Perry was rather suspicious of the new baby. It was nothing like any other animal she had ever seen. When I put the lion cub next to her, Perry growled and tried to run away. She had to be held down by force. But gradually she got used to the strange nursling and began to wash it, which meant she had adopted Kinuli. There was no longer any danger that Perry would hurt or abandon her. And when strangers came up to them Perry would even give an anxious growl, as if afraid someone would hurt the cub. The dog had no puppies at the time, but the maternal instinct was suddenly aroused in her.

Kinuli now slept in a drawer of the wardrobe. I still put a bottle of hot water in her bed at nights, but I did not feed her so often. She began to grow—very slowly, it is true. I no longer feared that she would not live, the most dangerous period was over. I began going back to work again for an hour or two at a time. Masha was as cross as ever, and when I went out I left junior assistants to keep watch over the cub.

Kinuli opened her eyes when she was six days old. First the left eye, then the right. Her eyes were mere slits, and very bleary. Her ears began to stand up and her bright crimson lips turned paler. Kinuli always knew me. Whether she was drinking milk, sleeping, or resting beside Perry, I only had to stretch out my hand towards her and she would leave whatever she was doing, and crawl over to me.

My little boy Tolya followed every movement of the cub. "Look, Mummy, look! Miaow-Miaow is licking my finger!" "She's crawling, Mummy, she turned her head." Tolya was quite offended when I named the cub Kinuli. "But *we* love her, *we* haven't abandoned her!" he objected. "Let's call her Miaow-Miaow, or Blue Eyes." Kinuli's eyes really were blue. So blue that the iris could hardly be seen. Kinuli did not see well. When she went about the room she blundered into everything. She would bump her head against the leg of a chair, and, not knowing how to get round it, would stand still for some time and then turn back. Kinuli waddled like a duck. Her paws got in her way and when she fell it was not on her side, but straight on to her back, like a mechanical toy.

AN EXTRAORDINARY LODGER

Letters came to me every day from all over the Soviet Union. Children, old men, women wrote to me. People of all sorts of professions and occupations. They sent addressed envelopes for a reply, they sent their photographs, and poems about Kinuli, and they all asked for an answer.

The questions they asked!

Some were afraid Kinuli would eat us up. They asked how she behaved in the house and how long I intended to keep her. They asked me to talk about her more often over the radio and to be sure to write a book about her. There were even animal-lovers who asked where they could get another lion cub to bring up and, if this was impossible, what animal I advised them to adopt.

At first I tried to answer these letters, but I soon had to give up the attempt. There were so many of them that there was no room for them in our letter box and the postman complained that he worked for us alone.

Newspaper reporters were interested in Kinuli too. They visited us almost every day. They photographed Kinuli eating, drinking, sleeping, and having her fur washed by Perry.

Masha still grumbled about Kinuli, but not so much as before. She even began helping me, and one day suddenly told me not to call in assistants from the Zoo any more. "You trusted me with your child.

and now you're afraid to trust a pest like that to me. Don't be afraid, I can look after it just as well as they can." And Masha really did look after Kinuli very well. She fed her strictly at regular hours, as she had fed Tolya when he was a baby. Her dishes shone, and the napkins she wiped the cub with were always freshly laundered. When Kinuli drank milk she braced her paws against Masha's hands, leaving deep scratches, but this did not make Masha angry. She even made diapers for Kinuli, and started calling her a tadpole instead of a pest.

The cub certainly had a very big head, its legs were short and thick, its body long. At first all its cries sounded the same to me, but soon I began to notice differences in them. 1 learned to know all Kinuli's moods from her cries—what she wanted, how she felt.

One day Kinuli fell ill. I noticed this while she was still quite jolly. My family laughed at me, telling me it was only my imagination. But I turned out to be right. The next day Kinuli lay in her bed and would not eat. She was ill for ten days. All that time I hardly slept at night, and kept jumping up, listening to her breathing, renewing the hot-water bottles. The neighbours would tap gently on the door in the mornings to ask how the invalid was.

When Kinuli recovered and got a little bigger I began letting her go out of the room. She walked calmly about the passage, bath-room and kitchen, and everyone stepped carefully, so as not to tread on her. Kinuli knew them all. She even had her likes and dislikes. She visited her favourites in their rooms, and showed them great affection; others she hissed at—especially one woman who had a loud harsh voice which the cub did not seem to like. Kinuli knew the footsteps of everyone in the flat. One neighbour went away while Kinuli was quite tiny, and came back when she was two months old. When Kinuli heard her footsteps she started, slunk to the door with her ears twitching restlessly, and listened for a long, long time.

Kinuli knew my voice, my step, and the smell of me. The moment I came into the room she would run to me and start rubbing herself against me.

Kinuli was very high-spirited and loved playing. Sometimes the children would come to see her, and stand outside the door, whispering into the keyhole: "Kinuli! Come here, Kinuli!" And Kinuli would leap up as if she understood and rush to the door. Getting on to her hind legs she would tug at the handle with one of her front paws, open the door, and bound into the passage. But there was no one to be seen—the children had hidden. Kinuli would start looking for them. She looked everywhere—in the bath-room, behind the doors, in the hall.

When she had found them it was her turn to hide. Her favourite place was behind the wardrobe. It was a tight fit, and she could hardly squeeze into it. The children knew where the lion cub hid, but they knew they must not find her too soon or she would be offended, and refuse to play. The children would wander about, laughing and pretending they could not find her. "Where's Kinuli?" they would ask

one another. "What's become of Kinuli?" And they would go on looking for her till she bounded out herself.

Their favourite game was "lion-hunting." The children would go out into the passage and form two groups, one at each end, and Kinuli stayed in the middle, lying low and waiting. Then Yura would run ever so fast past the cub. Kinuli would jump at him, like a cat at a mouse. If she caught him by the leg it meant the hunter was killed, if she only touched him, he was wounded, and if he got away, Kinuli had lost the game. But she very seldom lost, and when she was bigger she never missed—no one was quick enough for her.

Kinuli had lots of fun with the children. And how she pined when they went to the country for the summer! Tolya and Masha went away, too. Tolya wrote from the train: "Dear Mummy, I don't know whether to go on or come back, it's so dull without Kinuli." It was dull for Kinuli, too. She was used to romping and playing all day long, and now when I went to work she was alone with Perry, who was a quiet dog, and not very playful. Then I decided to bring a baby lynx as a companion for Kinuli.

TASKA

Like Kinuli, Taska was born in the Zoo. Her mother, a big yellow lynx, still lives there. For the first two months she looked after her babies conscientiously, washing them, feeding them, and pouncing threateningly at the bars of the cage if any visitor ventured too near. The baby lynxes developed splendidly. They could already eat meat, and would come out of their house and play. When they did this a crowd would collect in front of the cage. Everyone wanted to watch the little creatures' gambols, and tried to get as near as possible, and perhaps this was why the mother started dragging her babies about. She picked one of them up in her teeth and dashed about the cage with it. The baby struggled and cried, the visitors shouted, but she would not drop it. By the time an attendant ran up it was too late—the baby lynx lay dead on the floor, and the mother had picked up the next one, which the attendant got away from her with great difficulty.

One of its front paws was broken, and there was a film over its injured eye. It was the weakest of all the baby lynxes, a puny, miserable little creature. It would hide in the house and stay there all day long.

The baby lynx was in such a wretched state that I decided to take it home. The next day, after obtaining the director's permission, I wrapped the baby up in a robe and carried it off. As I walked up the stairs to the door of my flat I could not help wondering what my reception would be. When I came into the room, Shura (my husband) looked up as if wondering what I had brought home this time. When I produced the baby lynx he fairly yelled at me: "What's that little horror? Isn't a lion enough for you? You'll be bringing an elephant home tomorrow." This was too much for me. "In the first place, it's not a horror, it's a lynx. In the second place if the room were a little bigger I would certainly bring an elephant!" Shura made no reply, but only turned away with a despairing gesture. The next minute, however, he began to help me make a place for the lynx.

We put it in a box, with a saucer of milk and some meat beside it, and then we covered the box with boards. The neighbours were told nothing about the new nursling. They were used to Kinuli and fond of her, but who could tell what they would say to a lynx?

27

As for my husband, he asked me all about lynxes, and then declared he would adopt the baby lynx. He would name it, look after it, tame it—if, of course, I had not deceived him, and it really was a lynx. The next morning Shura got out of bed as soon as it was light, and hastened to have a look at his new baby. He was greatly disappointed. The little lynx was not nearly so affectionate as he had thought it would be. During the night it had gnawed at the sides of its box and spilled its milk—the meat it had left untouched. When Shura put out his hand to stroke it, the baby lynx retreated into a corner and growled. And he was equally unlucky about a name for it. It was extremely difficult to find one. We had a long and heated argument. My husband wanted to call the baby lynx Murka or Muska, and I wanted to call it Taskali,* because its mother had dragged it over the floor. We settled on Taska—northern Taska.

UNFORTUNATE INTRODUCTION

Kinuli took the greatest interest in the box from which such strange sounds and smells came. She even lost her appetite. She walked round and round the box, sniffing at it, and when I lifted a board to put some food in for the lynx, Kinuli tried to peep inside. As she was a great deal bigger than the lynx I was afraid she might hurt it, and I put off introducing them to one another. But I need not have worried.

One day I forgot to cover the box, and the moment I turned away Kinuli appeared and stuck her head in the opening. The lynx was terrified. It tried to hide in a corner, and growled, but Kinuli took no notice of this. The lynx hissed and growled, but still Kinuli took

* From the verb *taskat*—to drag.— *Tr.*

28

no notice. Then the lynx, driven to despair, its eyes round with fright, suddenly leaped up and thrust its claws and teeth into the lion cub's muzzle. Kinuli was so astonished that she made no attempt at resistance, and fled roaring from the room and along the passage, without a backward glance. She only recovered her senses in the kitchen, where she strode up and down, lashing her tail from side to side and mewing nervously. In the meantime the baby lynx had gone back to its corner where it stayed huddled up as if nothing had happened.

On the evening of that day a cage was brought from the Zoo, and the lynx cub was put into it. Taska did not like her new home. In the box there had been a dark corner to retreat to, to hide from people in, but here she was on view all the time. She gnawed at the bars, trying to break her cage and get away. All night long she uttered loud harsh cries, and in the morning the neighbours, who were not in the secret, asked me what animal I had taken in now.

The next night Taska made still more noise. Her cries could even be heard out-of-doors. We covered the cage with a carpet, a blanket, a mattress and some pillows. In fact, all my bedclothes were used, but the sound of Taska's cries came through them and kept everyone awake. Then I put the cage out on the balcony, where it was quieter and where nobody ever went. But Taska was still afraid. She started at every rustle, every sound, and tried to hide, and when any of us cleaned her cage she would jump at our hands, scratching and biting.

What didn't I do to try and tame the little savage! I fed her with my own hands, spent all my leisure time with her, and when I had to leave her I turned on the radio for Taska to get used to strange sounds.

She soon got tamer, however, no longer flying at an outstretched hand, and even allowing herself to be touched.

AT LIBERTY

We decided to let Taska out of her cage, to see what she would do. No one knew how a three-month-old savage from a cage in the Zoo would behave when it found itself in a room. Would Taska come out cautiously and hide, or would she dash about and look for a way of escape? I was very nervous. My hands actually shook as I opened the door of the cage. Then I moved away and waited. Taska sat there motionless, but the expression of her eyes became keener and she seemed to become tense. Then she relaxed, stretched, got up, and moved stealthily towards the door. For a long time she could not bring herself to cross the threshold. She put first one paw out, then another, listened, looked round. It was quite funny to watch her. She could easily have jumped out and run away, but instead she lingered in the doorway. I was just going to give her a shove when Taska suddenly stepped forward, and retreated. You might have thought her soft paw had touched a red-hot stove, and not a carpet, so terrified was Taska. Everything was new and alarming for her. She took a few cautious steps over the carpet and stopped. Further on, came the parquet floor—gleaming, slippery, unfamiliar. Taska advanced and retreated several times. She was very, very careful, this little lynx. You might have thought she was in a dense forest and not in a room, and that danger lay in wait for her everywhere.

It took her some time to get used to her new situation. But liberty did its work, and very soon Taska changed out of all knowledge.

She was here, there and everywhere. There seemed to be not a single place she could not get into. She jumped from one cupboard to another, clambered over picture frames, and once actually scrambled out through the *fortochka** and on to the ledge of the next-door window.

* Small ventilation pane in window.—*Tr.*

In fact, she behaved as if she were living in a forest and not in a room. Soon she was bigger than her brothers in the Zoo. Her paws straightened out, her eyes became clear, and her coat shone like silk. Even her character changed. Formerly, when I came into the room she would hiss and hide under the wardrobe. Now she ran to meet

me, rubbed herself against my legs and purred. She purred exactly like a cat, only louder.

I fed her on boiled semolina, eggs and meat. And how she loved meat! It was her favourite food. She knew quite well when the time came round for her to have it. She became restless, hung around the door, uttered cries, and the moment I came into the room, rushed up to me, deftly catching the bits thrown to her in mid air with one paw, and tossing them into her mouth. She always ate her food under the wardrobe.

Before eating the meat she played with it—tossing it up or pushing it away from her and running after it, and the bit of meat seemed to come alive between her paws.

Taska was alone for a long time and I could see she was lonely. She ran after me like a little dog, and when I went out of the room squealed shrilly. This was no longer the fierce beastie which had lost its mother, but a baby lynx, and like all little children it wanted companions. Then I made up my mind to try and make it up between Taska and Kinuli.

INCOMPATIBLES

Kinuli came into the room as if there had never been any lynx cub there. She went up to the edge of the carpet with a firm confident step, and lay down. Remembering the first unlucky introduction, which had ended in a fight, I kept an old towel in readiness, but it was not needed. The round roguish head of Taska peeped out from beneath the wardrobe, and her eyes followed the movements of the lion cub with by no means ill-natured curiosity. The behaviour of these animals, so alike, and yet so different, was interesting to watch. Kinuli lay quite still, nothing but her eyes moving, while Taska kept running past, touching her with her paw now and again, but if the lion cub so much as stirred, Taska darted under the wardrobe.

From now on I let them be together every day. Kinuli evidently had not forgotten the insult. She behaved as if she did not notice the lynx, while Taska now wanted to make friends, but they did not make friends for a long time. Many days passed before my nurslings began to play together. At first they were very cautious, not touching each other, keeping at a distance. Taska would come bounding out from beneath the wardrobe, rush violently at the lion cub as if she were just going to knock it down, but at the last moment stop and utter something like an abrupt "h'm." This was quite an affectionate sound. It is the sound the mother makes when she calls to her little ones, and Taska was telling Kinuli that she did not intend to hurt her.

I would often sit watching their movements, listening to the sounds they made, and trying to understand them. Sometimes I succeeded in this.

Why did Taska rush at the lion cub so noisily? Why did she always make for Kinuli's muzzle? Was it because she couldn't help it? Oh no! A lynx can slip past on its soft paws so quietly that the keenest ear cannot hear it, and it attacks its enemies from behind. But this was not an enemy. Nor was it a friend, either. They did not really know each other yet, did not trust each other. The lion cub might take fright, might strike, it must be warned. And Taska was warning. Watching them, I would say to myself: "These observations may come in handy. If I ever have to make friends with an animal I'll behave as they do." There is something to be learned from animals, too. I am always observing, always learning.

They came closer and more boldly up to one another every day. The usual game was for Taska to attack Kinuli. Deft and active, she would leap round the lion cub like a rubber ball. Nearer and nearer. And one day she jumped too far and fell on Kinuli. But no! I know Taska. She could not possibly have miscalculated. How many times, when I rolled a football on the floor, had she jumped straight on it from the table, spreading out her paws in mid air and never once jumping too far or too short! Had she miscalculated this time? I was quite sure she had done it on purpose. But how nervous they were! They sprang away from each other, as if they had burned themselves. All of a sudden their eyes were terrified, round, angry. There'll be a fight now, I thought. But the little creatures paused for a moment, then calmed down, and began playing. They were much more at their ease now. Sometimes one of them touched the other as if by chance, and then they stopped dead, looking searchingly at one another, and the game went on again.

That is how their acquaintance began. Acquaintance, not friendship. They were too different for that. Perhaps you are surprised at the idea of animals having incompatible temperaments. Is this really possible? Certainly it is. And yet I have known many animals quite different from one another, who got on very well.

Four wolves lived in the same cage with a goat, eating, playing, and sleeping together. They often quarrelled among themselves, but never with the goat. And yet Kinuli and Taska could not get on.

Kinuli was quiet, even a little sluggish. She loved playing, but there must always be something for her to seize on and worry. It was hard to rouse her to anger, but still harder to conciliate her, once she was angry. Kinuli remembered a grievance for a long time. If I hurt her feelings she would turn away in a huff, and not come up to me again for some days. Taska was quite different. She would flare up, attack and bite—and then it was all over. She was full of surprises. Nobody could ever tell what she would do the next minute, or even second,

Unlike Kinuli, Taska seldom showed affection. They played together very nicely, but never really understood each other, and they often had quarrels.

One day I gave Taska some meat. She grabbed at it and carried it up to Kinuli. Taska wanted to have a game before eating it. But Kinuli did not understand the hint. If you are given food, the thing to do is to eat it. She scooped up the meat with her paw, settled herself comfortably on the floor and started to eat her lunch. When Taska heard the crunching of the bones she was very much upset. Her slender body expressed astonishment in every line. What was the matter? Why had Kinuli done this? Taska had only brought the meat up to her for fun. She circled around Kinuli, watched her moving the jaws, listened to the crunching. She even tried to take the meat back, but Kinuli flattened her ears and gave such a roar that Taska leaped back, her eyes wicked and angry. I snatched up a towel in the nick of time. Taska could not endure the slight. She bristled all over and rushed at Kinuli with dog-like growls. I had to interfere.

Another time Kinuli was lying on the sofa with her tail hanging down. Taska took it for the velvet fringe on the sofa and bit so that it hurt. Again a quarrel. And this sort of thing happened several times a day.

CAN'T GET ON TOGETHER, CAN'T GET ON APART

It was always Taska who was the offender. She could not leave Kinuli alone, was always pulling her tail, or leaping round her. Poor Kinuli's head swam. She would hide under a chair, but Taska would jump on to the seat and aim at her from above. Sometimes Kinuli took offence and went back to her own room. But Taska would be after her in a minute. She never went straight into the room where Kinuli lived. First there appeared her shadow, long and narrow, then one pointed ear and a round eye. Then all these things disappeared, and a few minutes later Taska bounded into the middle of the room, uttering a friendly "h'm" as if nothing had happened.

Kinuli was bolder in her own room. She did not fear the lynx so much there, did not shrink into a corner, and if Taska teased her too much, did not hesitate to give her a box on the ear. Taska did not like this at all. The little rascal would try and lure Kinuli into her own room.

She was up to all sorts of tricks. Sometimes, tired of playing, she would pretend to be going away. Sticking up her stumpy tail she would make resolutely for the door. Kinuli would run ahead of Taska and try to stop her. Then Taska would lure her to the door of her own room, just for the sake of scratching her. They had to be separated with the help of a towel, the lynx driven back to her room, and Kinuli led away. Then they missed each other. Taska would scratch at the door and gnaw it with her sharp teeth, uttering cries that could be heard all over the flat. Taska's cries upset Kinuli. She would pace up and down the room, listening, and struggling to get back to Taska. I put them together again, and soon another quarrel began.

THE DEATH OF TASKA

It became more and more difficult with every day to keep the lynx in a room. She gnawed and tore everything she came across. She jumped about, squeezed herself in wherever she could, made a mess all over the place. We had long ago removed everything we could, but this did not prevent her from gnawing at the legs and backs of chairs, and tearing the upholstery of the sofa to pieces—even the carving on the bookshelves bore the marks of her sharp teeth. We had to consider taking Taska back to the Zoo. At first Shura would not hear of this, and asked me to leave Taska and send away Kinuli. But when Taska tore a new curtain and even managed to dirty a picture, he agreed to give her up.

A big, spacious cage was got ready for her at the Zoo. It was thoroughly scrubbed, the floor was strewn with sand, and a thick branch was put up in it for Taska to climb on to. Very soon an attendant was to come and fetch her away. But it was not to be.

One morning Taska did not rush to greet me when I went into the room, and did not answer when I called her.

It was strangely quiet in the room. So quiet that I was frightened. "Could she have jumped out of the window?" was my first thought. I took a few steps into the room and ... there was Taska lying in an unnatural posture near the sofa, a strip of fringe wound tightly round her throat. Perhaps she had got choked by the fringe while running past or playing with it; however that may be, the short life of little Taska had come to a sudden end.

ALONE AGAIN

Kinuli felt terribly lonely all by herself. There was no one for her to gambol with. She begged to be taken to Taska, cried, walked backwards and forwards past the closed door, even butted it with her head. But I would not let her into the room. It had first to be scrubbed, put in order, aired. The statuettes were put back, the curtains and draperies hung up, and the room became cosy once again. Nothing in it spoke of Taska. And yet I could not forget her, and whenever I went into the room I imagined I saw her long, narrow shadow. Kinuli remembered the little lynx, too. Three weeks later, when for the first time I let Kinuli into the room, she flew in as if the three weeks had not passed, as if the playful Taska were lurking behind every corner. But there was no Taska. Kinuli looked for her under the wardrobe, the table, the bed. She looked everywhere that the lynx could possibly have hidden, but she could not find her. Kinuli was left all alone.

The loss of her friend made Kinuli despondent. She had no appetite, lay down all day with her head between her paws, and very seldom got up.

We did our best to distract her. We bought a new ball, all sorts of toys. One of the neighbours gave her a pair of old slippers, another brought his gramophone to amuse her. There is something rather unusual in the combination of a lion and a gramophone. When it began to play Kinuli was terrified, and shrank into the farthest corner, refusing to come out. But curiosity won the day.

Kinuli gazed long at the unfamiliar object. She walked round it. Smelled it. Treated it as if it were alive. Tried to frighten it. Coming close up to it, she roared, stamped, and waited to see if the gramophone was afraid. But the gramophone was not a bit afraid and did not run away—just stayed where it was. Kinuli calmed down.

It was very curious to note her reaction to different tunes. She certainly knew them apart. Some she liked, others she did not. When the foxtrot "Life" was put on Kinuli came quite near and lay down. But suddenly a man's voice sang out. Kinuli looked over her shoulder and hissed.

She listened attentively to a waltz, but ran away as soon as the chorus struck up. She was afraid of many voices singing together, and always ran away from them on to the balcony.

The balcony was Kinuli's favourite retreat. If we chased her back into the room and closed the door she would get up on her hind legs and push at the handle with her front paws till the door came open. There was so much to interest her on the balcony. She could climb up on to a chair and watch the children playing in the yard, and the motor cars and horses coming in. From the second storey everything looked to tiny, ever so much smaller than it really was. There goes a motor-car just like Tolya's toy automobile that Kinuli used to play with! Kinuli would leap up and rush along the balcony after it.

But the car disappeared. Kinuli looked after it sadly, and the children down below laughed at her: "He gave you the slip, Kinuli!"

KINULI MOVES TO A NEW HOME

Soon after, my brother Vasya, whose room was next to ours, went away for his holidays. His room was big and full of light, with a balcony, and I decided to move into it temporarily with Kinuli and Perry. They took the move quite differently. Perry got under the table at once and went to sleep, but Kinuli walked about the room, sniffing at everything, inspecting everything. At last, her curiosity satisfied, she lay down. We spread a rug for her at the door, but she would have none of it and took up her quarters near the balcony door. I chased her away several times, fearing she would catch cold, but Kinuli always went back, and this became her favourite place.

She woke up very early, while we were still asleep. Shura and I slept on the balcony, and at the first sound of my voice Kinuli ran to the door and started mewing and scratching at it and pulling herself up to try and see me through the glass panels.

She very soon discovered what to do, however, and learned to push an armchair up to the door. It was a very heavy one, even I could hardly move it, but Kinuli found a way. She would back, run forward, and push it with her paws. Then she would back again, and give it another shove. When it was close against the door she jumped on to the seat and looked through the door. There she could watch me in comfort. She was afraid of Shura and left him alone. But she would always jump on to my bed, rubbing against my head, and inviting me to play with her.

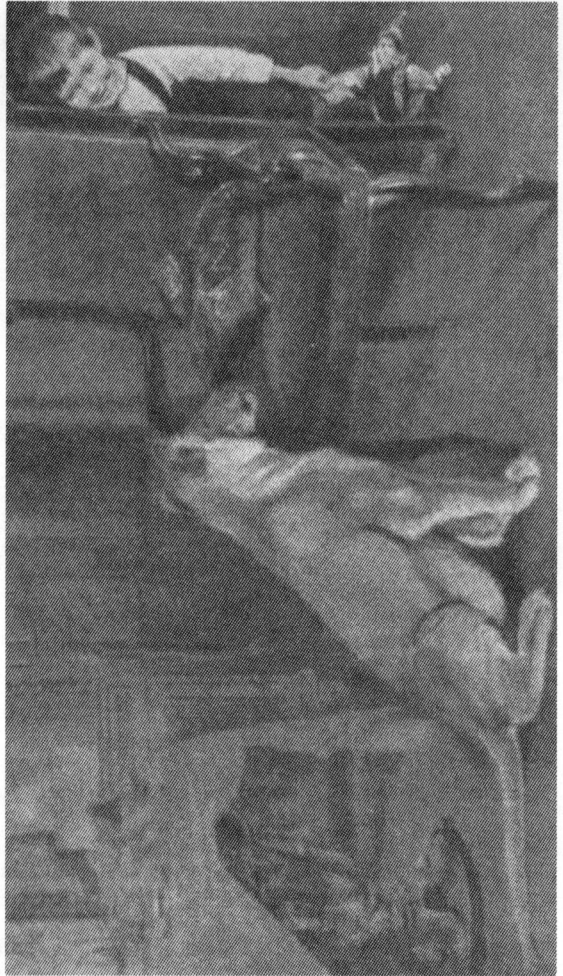

Very often, so as to get a little more rest, I would shut my eyes and pretend to be asleep, but it was no good. There was Kinuli, dragging the blanket off me. How she tormented me!

In the day-time, when the balcony was bathed in sunlight, Perry would come out to warm her old bones and Kinuli to watch the people in the street and take a sun-bath. She would lie right in the sun, always on her back, but she kept her head in the shade.

When the shade moved, Kinuli moved with it. She would lie a long time, for several hours, and I was very glad, for sunlight is good for baby beasts, too.

By now I was spending the whole day at work, only coming home during the lunch-hour to feed Kinuli.

As soon as I put the key into the lock Kinuli knew who it was. She met me at the door, jumping, rubbing against me. Sometimes she lay down at my feet, embracing them with her paws, and licking my shoes. She was even jealous of Perry, and would never let her come to me to be stroked. As soon as I put out my hand Kinuli got between us. Perry was a wise, self-controlled dog and always gave in. She would wag her tail from afar and go away. But not Kinuli. She would not eat if you did not first stroke her. Sometimes I was in a hurry to go back to work, my lunch-hour was nearly over, but I had to stay to stroke and pet her. Then I thought to myself: why tire myself out? I'll ask Xenia Stepanovna to look in on Kinuli while I am away, and feed her.

Xenia Stepanovna had been our neighbour for a long time. She was seventy-six and we all called her Granny. She was a good-natured old woman, always ready to oblige, and everyone loved her. Kinuli, too, soon grew very fond of her. The second time she saw her she got into her lap as she sat down, and began playing. Sometimes she accidentally tore her stocking or her apron, but Granny was never cross. She even tried to keep this from me, in case her pet should get a scolding. She loved Kinuli. Sometimes she gave her an extra drink of milk, always washing the saucer carefully afterwards.

But still I worried when I was away. Supposing Kinuli opened the balcony door, got out and fell into the yard? The railings were very wide apart, and the cub could easily get through them. When I left the house, I always tried the door several times to see that it was properly closed. I remember the fright I got once. When I went into the room Kinuli was nowhere to be seen, and the balcony door was

42

open. My hands and knees shook, I was afraid to look over the bal-cony—what if Kinuli lay dead in the yard? And all the time she was hiding behind the door. She had only wanted to play hide-and-seek, but she could not keep it up long, and as soon as I turned my back she jumped at me, butting me with her muzzle and rubbing against me.

After this we stretched wire netting in front of the railings, to be on the safe side.

Kinuli knew the exact hour when I ought to be back from work. She would wait nervously, listening to every sound. Because of her I could never go anywhere. Once I went to the country for two days, and when I came back I found everyone in great perturbation. Kinuli had eaten nothing all the time I was away. And how glad she was to see me! She would not let me out of sight the whole day long. If I went to the door, Kinuli went after me and clasped my ankles in her paws to prevent me going out. Granny looked at her and shook her head: "You mischievous imp! You only want to run after your mammy!" Naturally she did—who else was there for her to play with? In the winter there had been the children, but now they were all away, and Kinuli was bored. True, there was Perry, but Perry was no playmate—she slept all day long under the table. Kinuli would try to pull her out by the tail, or reach at her with a paw, but Perry only turned over and went to sleep again.

GOING FOR WALKS

When Kinuli was three months old I decided to start taking her for walks. I made a kind of harness from a leather strap and put it on her ever so gently. I had never imagined she would be so angry when the collar confined her neck. She was simply terrified. She roared, strained at the leash, then began tugging at the leather with her teeth, and of course the more she tugged the tighter grew the collar. Kinuli was in a frenzy. She rolled on the floor, growled, beat the air with her paws. I had the greatest difficulty in taking off the collar, and even then she dashed about the room and could not calm down. An hour later I put the harness on her again. Very gently, tickling her tummy, I fastened the buckle. Kinuli tried to wriggle out of the collar, but it did not worry her so much as before, and she soon quieted down. A few minutes later, Kinuli, Perry and I were out in the street.

Kinuli was terrified. From the window everything had looked so tiny and far away and now it was all so big and terrifying. At first the poor little thing was almost paralyzed with fear, but soon she began to struggle and scratch and cry in her efforts to get free. She lay on her back, refusing to move, or she darted suddenly to one side, dragging me after her. Not to frighten her more than I could help, I gave her as much freedom as possible, going wherever she pulled me, and doing my best to quieten her down with caresses. Perry tried as hard as I did. The wise old dog helped in her own way. She walked quietly beside Kinuli, as if they were in double harness, and when Kinuli seemed particularly upset, or came to a stop, Perry licked her muzzle and gave her a gentle shove with her nose.

And so gradually, day by day, we trained Kinuli to go for walks. I deliberately took her into the street, so that she should get accustomed to noises and people, and should not grow up such a wild creature. And very soon she really did get used to the noise of the street. She walked beside me like a big, docile dog, so quietly that people did not always notice her.

But if anyone *did* see that she was a lion, what a to-do there was! In less than a second we were surrounded by interested spectators. It was usually the militiaman who came to our rescue. He would appear

44

suddenly, make his way towards us, take a good look at the strange beast, and enter upon his duties. This, however, was no easy matter. The crowd would only disperse after we had taken shelter in a doorway. Sometimes we came across dogs in our walks. Every dog behaved in its own way. Some rushed at Kinuli barking furiously, others instantly took to their heels, but none of them dared to touch her. One day we met a woman with a dog trotting beside her. It was a snub-nosed lap-dog, with short legs and long silky hair. It walked solemnly beside its mistress with a blue bow on its neck.

Suddenly it caught sight of Kinuli. It probably took her for a big dog. It growled, stood still, and then plunged forward with furious barking and flung itself upon Kinuli. It discovered too late that this was no dog.

Poor little doggie! You should have seen it! Its perky aggressiveness turned to dismay, its eyes bulged with terror, but it could not turn back, and ran squealing full tilt into Kinuli. It fell back, but was up in a moment, and tore off madly, galloping along the middle of the road with its tail between its legs, and its mistress running after it, trying in vain to overtake it.

Kinuli gazed in mild surprise after the blue bow till it disappeared round a corner, then, turning her head lazily, she yawned and continued her walk with slow dignity. Kinuli could not walk very long. After about an hour and a half she would beg to be taken home. She knew the way to our flat and would bound swiftly up the stairs and scratch at the door.

After a walk Kinuli's appetite improved. She got eggs for breakfast. She would pick up her bowl in her teeth and bring it to me. I would break the eggs into the bowl and place it in front of Kinuli. Perry had her breakfast at the same time. They ate side by side, each from her own bowl. Kinuli always finished first. She would clean up the empty bowl with her tongue, which was as rough as a nutmeg grater, but she never attempted to take Perry's food away from her. Perry ate slowly, taking a long time over her meal. When she had finished she would go just as slowly up to the lion cub and lick its muzzle clean. Then they would both take a nap, lying side by side.

FOUR-LEGGED FILM STAR

My friends often asked me if Kinuli had ever been filmed. "Why," they said, "perhaps this is the only case of a lion being brought up in a house! What a pity she hasn't been filmed!" And I was sorry, too, of course. There was so much of interest, it would have been so nice to have it all filmed. But I had no camera and I did not know where to go to have a film taken. But an opportunity soon presented itself, however. A film was being made in the Zoo. When the producer learned that I had a lion in my flat he offered to film it. Needless to say I gladly gave my consent.

The producer wrote a scenario and came on a day when I did not go to work, to shoot the film. The cameraman brought the film and camera, the producer a tripod and a funny sort of box. Loaded from head to foot, they appeared for the first time in our flat. After relieving themselves of their burdens, they went to make the acquaintance of the "star."

Kinuli received the newcomers with distrust. She sniffed for a long time at their clothes and boots before allowing herself to be touched. It was impossible to film her that day. Kinuli needed time to get accustomed to the strangers before she could get rid of her fear of them and be at her ease. And so the cameraman and the producer sat on the floor for hours tempting her with bits of meat and trying to win the confidence of the four-legged "star." This was very, very difficult. When I was there Kinuli took no notice of them, when I went out of the room she would not go near them, and would not even take meat from their hands. But in the end they won—Kinuli was no longer shy and the filming could begin.

Everything was set up beforehand. The camera was screened off by a row of chairs with a blanket hung over them. The cameraman hid behind this screen. It was the only way, for though Kinuli was tame she was still as suspicious as a wild beast. When everything was ready Kinuli and Perry were let into the room. Perry had to be there to keep Kinuli calm—without Perry, Kinuli would not have played. According to the scenario she had to lie quietly on the sofa. She jumped on to it willingly enough, but the rattling noise of the camera alarmed her, and she ran away. And here our troubles began. Kinuli simply would not be filmed. We could not make her come nearer. Neither scoldings nor pleadings were any good. Some way of drowning the noise of the camera had to be found.

Suddenly I remembered that Kinuli was very fond of music, and would lie for hours beside the gramophone, quite oblivious to what was going on around her. So we put the gramophone next to the camera. The familiar sounds of dance music drowned the rattling of the camera and Kinuli at once felt at her ease. She played, ate, drank, lay on the sofa, and did everything she was asked to. The cameraman was delighted. He photographed Kinuli, while the producer wound up the gramophone and changed the records.

There was not enough light in the room to take good photographs. The sun moved and we had to follow it with tables, chairs, "star," and all. Then Kinuli would not pose, or the camera was in the wrong place. In fact we had nothing but trouble. And things were no better with Perry. They did manage to film Kinuli, with the aid of music, but nothing could be done with Perry. She had once been photographed by flashlight and terrified by the flash. Ever since, the moment she caught sight of a camera she would lie on her back, shut her eyes, and play possum.

But gradually all the difficulties were overcome. Kinuli was filmed eating, playing with Perry, bringing her bowl, drinking milk from a bottle. She was filmed in the yard, playing with the children. They were fortunate to get a picture of Kinuli with her bottle, for a few days later she swallowed the rubber nipple.

NO MORE RUBBER NIPPLES!

I came back from work one day to be greeted at the door by Granny, with the tearful exclamation:

"Vera Vasilyevna! Oh, my dear! The nipple!"

I couldn't understand what she was trying to tell me.

"What's the matter? What nipple?" At last I managed to get at the truth. Kinuli had pulled the nipple off the bottle and swallowed it.

"Before I could turn round—" said Granny, weeping.

In spite of this, Kinuli felt splendid, gambolling and playing as usual. But I could not help worrying. Who could say how it would end? I had seen many cases of animals dying after swallowing rubber articles. Rubber cannot be digested. It swells inside, sometimes causing a stoppage, and the animal dies. The same thing might happen to Kinuli. Besides, Kinuli could not drink milk from a saucer, or rather she would not. She lapped up soup or porridge from her bowl beside Perry, with the greatest of ease, but simply refused to drink milk except from a bottle. A nipple had to be bought in a hurry. But Kinuli would not use it. The moment she felt it in her mouth she spat it out, sniffed at it and turned away.

I lost my temper, picked up the naughty little thing and stuffed the nipple into its mouth. But Kinuli wriggled out of my grasp, spat out the nipple, would not keep it in her mouth for a moment. I understood what was wrong. The old nipple had felt, smelt and tasted quite different. Kinuli was used to it and behaved to the new one as if it were a new mother. Try as I might boiling it first in water, to soften it, then in milk, to take away the taste of rubber, she would not have it. Kinuli cried with hunger, would not eat meat, and would not drink milk from the new nipple.

Three days passed, and for three days Kinuli ate nothing. And only on the fourth day, when she was really hungry, did she begin to drink milk from the new nipple. But she did not have it for long. The very next day she swallowed it, too. It was her last rubber nipple, for after this I never bought any more. And gradually Kinuli learned to drink milk out of a basin.

50

MAKING FRIENDS

Tolya, Masha, and my brother Vasya came back from the South in September. I went back to my own room, intending to take Kinuli with me, but she had got so used to Vasya's room that she didn't want to go. She would come into our room, play about for a little while, and ask to go back, scratching at the door and crying to be let out. We had to ask Vasya to let Kinuli live in his room. Vasya consented. He loved animals and didn't mind keeping a lion cub a bit. But the cub minded. Kinuli disliked strangers intensely. And here was a stranger intruding in *her* room. (Kinuli considered the room hers.) Vasya's arrival disturbed her peace and Kinuli took a strong dislike to him. She expressed it in her own way. Even my brother's things annoyed her.

The first day it was his suitcase which suffered. Vasya left it on the floor when he went to see us. When he got back the suitcase was open, its contents scattered all over the floor. Kinuli had torn up one shirt and was beginning on another. Vasya tried to get it away from her but could not. Kinuli refused to give it up, snarling and striking out at his hand with her paw, her long, terrible claws unsheathed.

In the night it was no better. Vasya went to bed, and Kinuli walked round and round him, dragging off now the blanket, now the pillow, so that he could not sleep. Vasya gathered up his bed-clothes in a bundle and sat on them. He sat up all night, and the next night decided to sleep on the table. But that was not much better. When I came into the room I scarcely recognized it. The air was filled with feathers and down. There was a torn mattress on the floor, and Kinuli was finishing up the last of the pillows in a corner. What was to be done? My brother would be very angry when he came back. I rushed for a needle and cotton and started stitching everything up. It did not take me long, but it was no easy matter to gather up the feathers. I caught at them in mid air and stuffed them into the pillow-case, but they flew out again. I was exhausted, but what did Kinuli care? She ran after me, getting in my way, and thrusting her muzzle wherever she could. It was all good fun for her.

My brother once went out of the room, leaving his radio set, which he was repairing, on the table. Kinuli immediately jumped on to the table and knocked it off with her paw. When Vasya came back his set was nothing but a heap of chips.

There was no end to the things Kinuli spoilt. She tore up coats and curtains. Vasya dared not leave anything within her reach. When he was called to the telephone in the passage he had to take his bed-clothes with him. The neighbours would laugh at him: "'Your lodger doesn't give you much peace, does she?" But Vasya never got angry with his lodger. He was always patient and affectionate with the cub, and did everything to win her confidence. He had loved the little cross-patch from the very first day, and never lost an opportunity of stroking and petting her, very gently, so as not to alarm her.

I purposely saw less of her now, and Vasya looked after her and fed her himself. In about a fortnight Kinuli began to get fond of him. She did not go to him of her own accord, but she no longer snarled at him, and allowed him to touch her. It was a long time before she showed him affection. She began by going up to him, lying down at his feet, and every now and then rubbing her head against them, as if by accident.

But once Vasya went to the country and did not come home that night. Kinuli was greatly upset, running about the rooms, mewing and listening.

Vasya came back the next morning. Kinuli heard his footsteps in the passage. She got the door open and rushed to him, hugging his ankles with her paws, and rubbing against him for a long time.

Kinuli and Vasya became inseparable friends. Vasya hardly ever went out, and spent all his spare time at home. There was nothing he would not do to amuse Kinuli. He played ball and hide-and-seek with her. There was nowhere to hide, so he would get into the wardrobe, calling out: "Kinuli, where am I? Kinuli!" Kinuli would look every-where, listening, or would crouch, waiting. The moment Vasya stuck out his head she was there; jumping up to him, asking to be petted, catching at his legs. Vasya taught her to stay on the seat of a chair while he moved it about the room. Kinuli would jump on to the seat, leaning against the back of the chair. Vasya would move the chair about the room while she sat there, very dignified, looking about her proudly.

At that time Vasya was working at a factory. He got up early, at seven o'clock. Kinuli always waked him. Very carefully, with her claws sheathed, she would slap him with her paws, lick his hair and face. Her tongue was as rough as a nutmeg grater, and left a red mark on his skin. But Vasya bore it all and never forgot to pet her before going to work.

LION IN THE STREET

All through September the weather was bad. It rained most of the time, and if the sun did come out it was only for a few minutes. Kinuli could not go out. She stayed at home thoroughly bored, for there was no one for her to play and romp with. Perry lay under the table almost all day and when she did come out, crept back the mo-ment Kinuli began to tease her. But at last the sun came out again. We decided to take advantage of this and have Kinuli filmed out-of-doors.

We all got up early that day. I was nervous and Kinuli became infected with my nervousness. She refused her meat, fretted, mewed. By ten o'clock everyone was ready. The producer and cameraman had arrived.

Vasya, Kinuli, Perry and I were to go by car to the place settled upon for the filming, and the rest by the Metro (Moscow underground railway).

A taxi was waiting for us in the yard. When the driver saw me bring out a lion cub he cried out and slammed the door of his car. Not having been warned, he had certainly not expected such a passenger. Before he could recover from the shock, Vasya quickly opened the other door, helped Kinuli, Perry and me in, and himself got in beside the driver. The driver was so bewildered that he could not find a word to say. Bending over the wheel and glancing back nervously at the restless lion cub, he drove cautiously out of the yard. Kinuli was at first alarmed at the unaccustomed movement and the noise of the engine. She darted from the window to the door, trying to get out. Then she calmed down and began looking out of the window. The driver calmed down, too. All the way he kept asking me about Kinuli, her life at home, her temper, her habits. "You should write a book," he advised me. And when I told him I *was* writing a book he was still more interested.

We were so absorbed in our talk that we hardly noticed the distance to Kropotkin Street, where we were all to meet. The others had not arrived, and we had to wait for them. Kinuli lay quietly on the seat. She could not be seen from outside and nobody bothered us. Once a man came up to hire the taxi, caught sight of Kinuli and made off quickly, without looking back. We got out of the car when the others arrived and everything was ready for the filming. A lion cub so near the Metro station immediately attracted the attention of the passers-by, and in a few moments we found ourselves in the centre of a dense circle of inquisitive onlookers.

Kinuli made a terrific stir in the street. Conductors and drivers leaned out of their trams, the passengers jumped out. Children ran up from all directions.

But this was nothing to what awaited us in Petrovka Street.

The car had hardly stopped when a crowd surrounded us, and when we got out, the excitement was indescribable. The militiamen and street cleaners could do nothing. In the space of a minute the pavement, the whole street, was crowded. People looked out of windows, came out on to balconies, little boys shouted: "Lion ! Lion!"

All traffic was held up. Buses, taxis, and cars came to a stop. The drivers did not even try to go on. Newspaper reporters and amateur photographers sprang up from goodness knows where. Their cameras clicked, and it was impossible to start filming Kinuli.

Four times we pretended to go away, four times we skirted the street by side-streets and came back, but nothing could be done. With the greatest trouble a few feet showing Kinuli walking along the pavement were shot, and then we all went home.

The next day there was a notice in the paper: "An interesting sight could have been observed in Petrovka Street yesterday—the filming of the young lioness Kinuli." Then followed a description of the shooting. The paragraph ended: "The filming of Kinuli aroused great interest among passers-by. The car which took Kinuli back was escorted by bicycles, motorcycles, and motor-cars right up to the home of V. Chaplina, a member of the staff of the Zoo, who has brought up the cub from the day of its birth."

HOLIDAY

The film starring Kinuli was ready by the 7th of November, the anniversary of the Revolution. Our whole family was invited to the pre-view. Of course Kinuli and Perry were invited too. Since the time of the shooting Kinuli had been in a car several times, and when the taxi drove up to our door she got in by herself, settling comfortably on the seat and looking round placidly. But the driver wrapped his scarf round his neck before speeding off—this was a very alarming fare.

When we went into the auditorium everyone jumped up, crying: "The lion's come! The lion's come!" There was much shouting and excitement. But Kinuli did not turn a hair. She got on to a seat and lay down in a relaxed attitude.

The lights went out and the film projector began rattling. The unfamiliar sound alarmed our Kinuli, who gave a roar and turned towards the sound. Then she glanced at the screen, saw herself, and sat very, very still and alert. Perry looked, too, at first, but soon curled up and went to sleep. Kinuli responded to everything she saw on the screen. Suddenly she saw her own ball there. Her very own ball! This was too much for Kinuli, she jumped off the seat and was close up to the screen in a couple of bounds, jumping up to it, and trying to get hold of her beloved toy. I got her back with difficulty. Kinuli watched the rest of the picture attentively, never taking her eyes off the screen, and even after the lights were turned on continued to look at it. Then she stretched and yawned luxuriously.

That day she slept even more soundly than usual, though she started several times in her sleep and shifted her paws. Perhaps she was dreaming that she had caught the ball.

Then Kinuli and Tolya were invited to a children's matinée.

This time, too, things did not go quite smoothly. When the car came for Kinuli it turned out she was locked in her room. Hearing my voice she had tried, as usual, to open the Yale lock with her paw, but accidentally let the catch slip. The lock had to be broken.

The children greeted Kinuli with such loud cries of joy that she was terrified and rushed out and down the stairs again, almost knocking me over. It took me a lot of trouble to get her back into the hall. But now the children kept quiet and Kinuli recovered her composure. I sat down, Kinuli and Perry at my feet, and all round us the children. They examined every hair on the lion cub, its eyes, its powerful paws, its rounded ears. Kinuli was unusually calm and even allowed the children to touch her. The children lined up, gently stroking in turn the animal's soft fur.

The next day we treated Kinuli to a drive around Moscow as a reward for her good behaviour. We took her along the most interesting streets, showed her the festively decorated city and the illuminations.* Kinuli never took her eyes from the window all the time. At one point our taxi was overtaken by a car in which there were some foreigners. Seeing the lion they drove alongside of us for a long time, trying to show us by gestures that they recognized Kinuli.

We got home late. Kinuli had begun to show signs of nervousness, and the car had hardly drawn up in front of the house when she got the door open, and streaked up the stairs. Perry and I had difficulty in keeping up with her. I thought Perry was just as astonished as myself at the hasty flight of our nursling. And the nursling, who was already in the flat, almost knocked down a woman in the hall, and ran into the room, where she immediately squatted on her sand-box. She was very clean.

* In honour of November 7th, the anniversary of the Revolution.—*Tr.*

ILL

In the autumn Kinuli fell ill. Her illness was long and serious. She lay there very melancholy, eating nothing, and when she tried to get to her feet fell back with loud roars of pain. She only calmed down when we warmed her with an electric heater. She turned first one side to it, and then the other, and actually pulled it nearer with one paw, without burning herself. And yet Kinuli got worse every day.

A doctor was called. At first he was afraid to go into the room. The patient was a very unusual one—a wild beast, after all! Supposing it were to attack him? A place had to be screened off with chairs before the doctor would agree to go in. Kinuli was so ill that she simply did not notice him. She did not even open her eyes, and lay there on her side, breathing heavily. The doctor looked at her from a respectful distance, and advised dosing her with castor oil. He hurried away without so much as examining her.

We sent for other doctors. They each prescribed something different, but were all agreed on one point—Kinuli would not recover, whatever was done for her.

Kinuli's illness was reported in the newspapers. And the letters I got at that time, the questions put to me, the amount of advice I received, were something tremendous. Most of the letters came from children: "How is Kinuli?" "Is she getting better?" "What do the doctors say?" People kept coming to enquire after her. Complete strangers shared our anxiety. Even the children in the yard were less noisy than usual. I often heard them hushing a comrade who was making too much noise. They were continually running in to ask after Kinuli.

We did everything we could to save the cub. Someone was on duty the whole time. I forgot what sleep meant. I was almost dizzy with

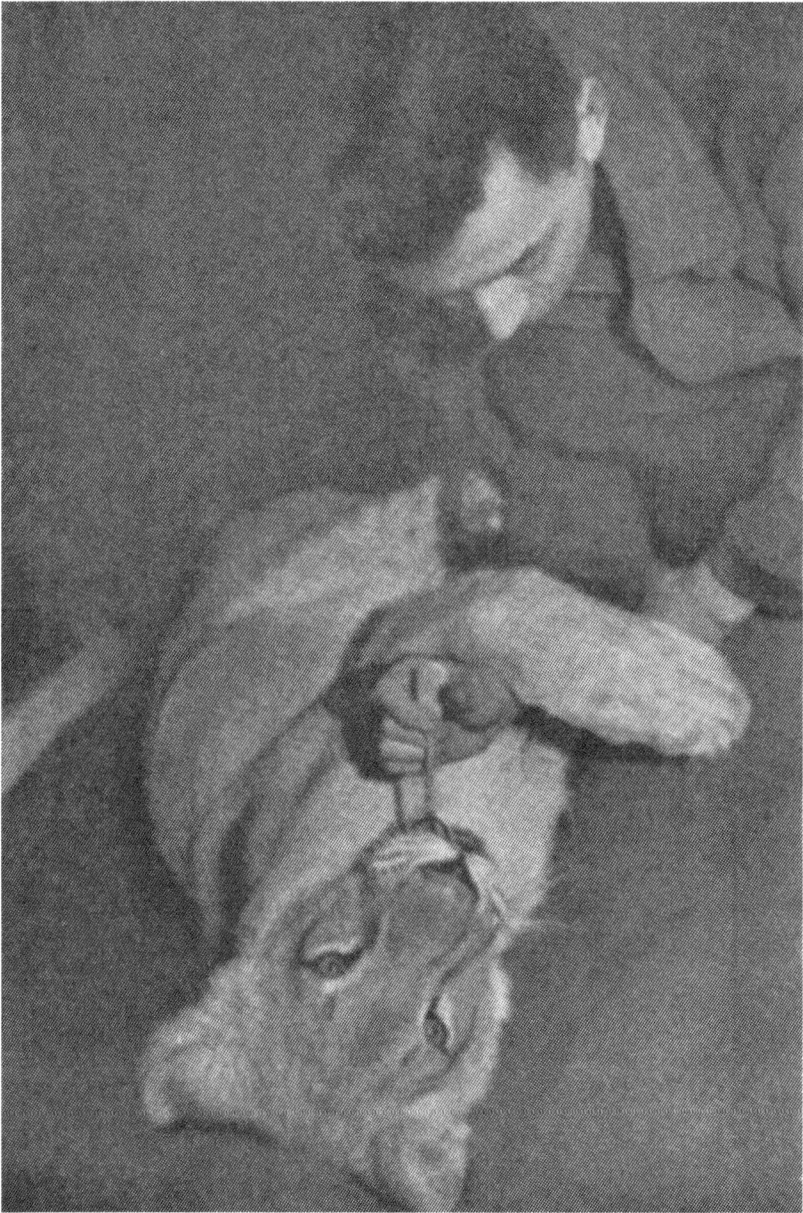

fatigue, and yet I could not go away and rest. If I so much as moved in the direction of the door Kinuli strained after me, mewing plaintively, as if she were calling out "ma-ma-ma." And every time I had to go back. The nights were interminable. It was perfectly still in the room, and nothing could be heard but the ticking of the clock and Kinuli's irregular breathing.

Kinuli was ill for three weeks. For three weeks she battled with death. For three weeks I had to feed her by force. With the utmost difficulty I would push a piece of meat into her mouth and try to get her to swallow it. Kinuli did not want to eat. She turned away her head and spat out the food. Sometimes we tried persuasion. The whole family pleaded with her—Vasya, Shura, even little Tolya.

"Eat, Pussy!" he begged her. "Just a tiny bit!" And added softly: "A teeny-weeny bit! All you have to do is to swallow it."

Whether our pleadings had their effect on Kinuli, or whether she simply wanted to get rid of us, I don't know, but she *did* eat—just a little.

We were aided in our efforts by a fly—an ordinary fly which was waked up by the warmth and started feeding beside Kinuli. It crept under her very nose and warmed itself at the electric heater. Kinuli detested this fly. The moment it appeared she would snarl angrily, hitting out at it with her paw, and actually ate to prevent her enemy getting the food—very little, it is true, but still it was something. Naturally we were delighted to have such an ally.

After a time Kinuli began to recover, very slowly. She still had a poor appetite and could not get up, but she began making attempts to play. She played chiefly with a wooden spoon and her ball. She rolled the ball with her nose, or clasped the spoon between her paws, lying on her back and holding it in front of her for a long time. It would be hard to say why these were the things she liked to play with most. We only had to say "ball" for her eyes to light up, and at the word "spoon" she lay on her back at once. Perry was the first to notice the signs of the cub's recovery. When Kinuli roared and writhed with pain the dog was afraid of her and hid under the table, refusing to go near her. But as soon as she began to get better Perry again came to sleep beside her, searched her coat solicitously for fleas, and washed her face. And when, one day, Vasya burst into the room and told us that Kinuli had torn his new trousers and a book left on the table, everyone was delighted, for it meant that Kinuli was well again.

KINULI GROWS UP

After her recovery, a new collar was made for Kinuli and I decided to take her out for a walk. I was afraid she would be very nervous after such a prolonged interval. But either because Kinuli had grown up, and people no longer seemed so big to her, or because she had become more sensible, she behaved very well, walking about the streets as quietly as Perry did.

I went into the yard with her. The children no longer greeted her as they used to. Some of the bravest held their hands out towards her, but mothers snatched up their babies and whisked them away. Inquisitive passers-by came into our little yard, asking the children and the neighbours about Kinuli. Exclamations of astonishment could be heard and the house manager was envied for having such a tenant.

The tenant had now grown very big and changed greatly. Kinuli's muzzle had lengthened, and was like a full-grown lion's. Her newly grown whiskers made her look quite different, and only two little moles and a tiny spot on her nose reminded us of the former Kinuli.

It was almost impossible, looking at her, to believe that this was that same little creature that could literally be held on the palm of one's hand. Now this "little" creature was bigger than Perry, and could hardly get under the table or sit on a chair.

But though she was now so big, her habits remained the same. She gambolled up to me as violently and affectionately as she used to when little bigger than a kitten. The only difference was that now I had to lean against the wall, or the caresses of the "kitten" might have knocked me over. Kinuli played very carefully with my hand, taking it right into her mouth or licking it, and never once did she hurt me. If she forgot herself for a moment I only had to raise my voice ever so little and she instantly dropped my hand.

Kinuli was remarkably sensitive to intonations. She might be up to some mischief, breaking something for instance, but if she heard Vasya's footsteps she would be under the table in a moment, and hide there, waiting to see what would happen. If Vasya came in in a bad temper and began scolding her, she would stay there, but if he seemed good-humoured she would spring up and put her front paws on his chest, or lie down and rub her head against his foot. She loved to lie with her head resting on our feet—mine or Vasya's. This was her favourite position.

In the evening, when everyone came back from work, we got up a regular circus in Vasya's room. We placed chairs against the walls for our friends. The table, as the safest place, was considered the boxes, and the gallery was in front. The programme included: "Lion Playing Football," "Wrestling, Riding on a Chair" and "Man Puts Head in Lion's Mouth." The last turn was thought to be extremely dangerous. It was Vasya's. He would lie on the floor, while the music stopped, just as it does in the circus, and Kinuli, embracing him cautiously between her paws, would lick his head.

This was the star turn of the programme and was always a tremendous success. Vasya would get up, I would turn on the radio, and the spectators would applaud noisily, while Vasya, his head sticky from the licking, would bow and give Kinuli an affectionate pat.

Vasya was very fond of Kinuli and she returned his affection, showing her devotion by all sorts of caresses. But sometimes Vasya turned her out of the room. Then Kinuli would be offended and come to me to complain, lying down and mewing ever so plaintively.

At other times she would complain of me to Vasya, and if we both scolded her, she would go to Perry. So Vasya called her a telltale and sometimes offended her on purpose to make her complain. It was very amusing to watch her.

Kinuli could swear, too. She croaked like a frog, and went straight to her place. Then we had to beg her pardon.

"Kinuli, Pussykins, I won't do it again," Vasya would say, and Kinuli, after holding out for a time, and turning away from him, always came round in the end.

There never was such an easy-going, affectionate creature! She would not even eat her meat till she was petted. But her behaviour to strangers was now quite different. She sometimes snarled at them, and if they turned their backs on her would even jump at them. This was only her fun, but the neighbours began to be afraid of her. Especially after she knocked Granny down.

This happened quite unexpectedly, even for Kinuli, who did not know her own strength. One day, when the old woman was washing the floor, Kinuli jumped at her, and Granny fell over. Kinuli, as frightened as Granny herself, gave a roar and fled from the room.

But another time it was Kinuli who saved the situation.

It happened on my day off. There was nobody in the flat, but a little girl called Galya, and myself. Suddenly there was a ring at the front door and Galya went to open it. A middle-aged man with a sack on his back came in. When we asked him what he wanted he said he had come to exterminate the bugs in our flat. It was no use assuring him that there were no bugs, that the neighbours would come back late, no use telling him to go. The "exterminator" firmly refused to go. I did not know what to do. I could not go away and leave him there alone, and I could not stand there all day either.

It was Kinuli who came to my rescue. She came slinking into the hall, saw a stranger, and stood frozen to the spot, fixing the keen steady eyes of a wild beast on the stranger's face. The man turned his head and suddenly his eyes met the motionless, sinister glance of a wild beast. Kinuli stretched, remained still for a second, showing the gleaming fangs of a half-grown lioness. The "exterminator" started, and made a timid move towards the front door. It was locked.

"Don't be afraid," said Galya, noticing his movement. "It's only a lion."

"A lion! Let me out, can't you?" he yelled.

Without waiting for a reply he snatched the key out of my hand, tore the door open, and rushed downstairs two steps at a time.

We never saw the "exterminator" again.

But after this something else happened.

THE CASE OF THE BURGLAR

One day I came back early from work. I found the front door unlocked and Kinuli roaming about the passage.

I was astonished. What could it mean? Who could have let her out of the room? We never locked the door, but everyone knew there was a lion in our room, and nobody would go in when we were not at home. "Who could have let Kinuli out?" I wondered. I went in and the first thing I saw was a stranger perched on the top of the side-board. His face was covered with red blotches, his eyes darted from side to side, and he was shaking all over.

Strangers were always coming to look at our lion, and so I was not surprised to see him. Still, to make sure, I asked him:

"How did you get in, Comrade?"

The "Comrade," his teeth chattering with fear, replied:

"That lion of yours chased me here."

"Very well," I said. "You've been there long enough. Now come down."

But he was not going to do this! He only squeezed nearer and nearer to the wall.

"M-m-militia!" he said. "Call the militia!"

I kept telling him to come down, but he only repeated again and again: "The militia!"

There was nothing for it but to comply with his request and call up the militia station. They soon came. Hardly had the militiamen got into the room, when the "comrade" rushed up to them, hiding behind them, and begging them to take him away at once.

A few days passed. I had forgotten all about the incident when a notice appeared in *Izvestia.*

It came under the heading of topical events and gave a detailed description of the case of the burglar. I quote the notice in full, without any changes:

"Not long ago we reported that V. V. Chaplina, director of the young animals' department in the Moscow Zoo, was bringing up the lion cub Kinuli in her home.

"Kinuli is now a handsome young lioness, about the size of a Great Dane. She opens doors by pulling at the handle with her paw, and when she is hungry she picks up her bowl in her teeth and goes to the kitchen.

"A few days ago V. V. Chaplina, returning from work, found Kinuli in a state of great excitement, lying on the threshold of her room and thumping the floor angrily with her tail. Her skin twitched nervously, she was gazing upwards fixedly. Following her glance, Comrade Chaplina saw an unknown man perched on the top of a high cupboard. He was trembling with fear and looking wildly round.

"Refusing to quit his refuge the stranger told his story without getting off the cupboard. He had broken into the house for purposes of burglary, and had gone undisturbed from room to room in the empty flat till he came to the one in which Kinuli was. The burglar was well into the room before he noticed that he was in the presence of a lioness.

"The law-breaker involuntarily backed towards the door, but Kinuli stood in his way, roaring ominously. He climbed on to the table, and she went after him there. The unfortunate burglar jumped on to the top of a high cupboard, and remained there for over two hours, zealously guarded by the formidable beast."

The paper containing this notice came out early in the morning, while I was still asleep. I was roused from my slumbers by the telephone. I picked up the receiver. The voice of a friend came to my ears:

"Vera Vasilyevna, are you still alive?"

"Yes, thank you," I replied. "Why?"

"Why? Havent you seen the paper? You haven't? Oh, you must! It's written there that a burglar broke into your flat and Kinuli drove him on to the top of a cupboard and almost ate him up. My wife and I were very worried, so I thought I'd ring up to find out how you are."

I had to tell him the whole story from beginning to end, and hardly had I put down the receiver when there was another ring.

So many people wanted to know what had happened to me, that almost as soon as I hung up the receiver the bell rang again. It never stopped. The harassed and irritated neighbours did not go to it any more, and a few hours later I escaped from the house.

But my troubles were not over in a single day. The newspaper had given not only my name, but my address.

Letters came by the hundred, and we had many new visitors. Masha opened the door to them from morning to night. It wasn't so bad in the day-time, but in the evening we could neither work nor rest, our whole time went in opening and shutting the front door.

Again Kinuli came to the rescue. She had a habit of sniffing at the feet of people coming into the room. Or, still more alarming, she would put her paws round a visitor's ankle and give it a gentle nip. Kinuli's teeth were sharp and terrible, and a stranger could not tell whether she was not really going to bite. The poor dears would edge away and very soon take their leave. And gradually fewer and fewer people came to look at the lion.

LOVE TRIUMPHANT

Although Kinuli was now a grown-up lioness, the neighbours loved her as much as ever. For them she was still the little Kinuli whose mother had abandoned her. Everyone loved her—except little Galya's grandmother. And she did everything in her power to get rid of the lion.

She came to my flat one day, followed by nine or ten persons. Calling me out she took me aside, smiling. It appeared this was a sanitary commission. One of the doctors asked me:

"Is it true that you keep a lion in your room, Comrade?"

"It is," I answered. "What about it?"

"You see," he said, "there has been a complaint from some of the tenants that it makes dirt in the flat. So we've come to investigate."

Most of my neighbours were indignant.

"Complaint? Who from? Why, Kinuli's cleaner than a cat!"

I decided not to argue.

"Come in and see her," I said.

I opened the door, and the commission shrank back, hiding behind one another and staring.

Kinuli came to meet me, asking to be petted. Perry came up too. The commission, seeing that there was nothing particularly alarming, drew nearer, and the doctor, forgetting all about the state of the room, gazed at the lioness in admiration. Kinuli began to show off, lying on her back, rubbing against me, taking my hand gently into her mouth, as gently as if she really were a cat. And the room was perfectly clean, not a speck of dust anywhere. There was not even the slightest smell from the lioness. They put it all down in their notebooks.

But this did not discourage the old lady. She handed in another complaint, as if from all the tenants. I did not know what to do about it. Every day a new commission came. They sent scores of notices demanding the eviction of the lioness. And the old lady went about in triumph.

"The lion won't live here. I'll get rid of it."

But when the other tenants found out that a complaint had been made in their names they were furious.

"We'll stand up for Kinuli! We'll go in a body and tell them she isn't in our way."

And they wrote a statement to the militia:

"We, the tenants in flat number so-and-so, house number so-and-so, Bolshaya Dmitrovka Street, declare that we have nothing against the lion which lives in our flat. It is perfectly tame and is always kept locked up. It never goes into the passage, kitchen or bath-room, and the room in which it lives is kept clean and tidy. The lion never causes any trouble to us, the tenants of the flat, and is not noisy."

Everyone in the flat signed this statement, and one woman added a postscript to it:

"I have three children, seven, ten and eleven years old, and I see no danger for them in the lion's living in the flat. The animal is tame and is under constant care."

The whole flat rose to the defence of Kinuli.

News of the eviction of the lioness reached the legal authorities. Things took a different turn. One evening the house manager came to me with the head of the militia station. "Well," I thought, "she'll have to go." I took them into the room, but my feelings were too much for me, and I could not help bursting out:

"Are you going to evict her?"

"Oh, no!" they said. "We only want to find out what it's all about. We have received a statement from Sanitary Inspection that the other tenants complain of your lioness. They write that they're afraid to leave their rooms, and have to take sticks and other objects to defend themselves when they do. So we've come to investigate."

I invited them into my room and told them everything, and showed them the statement drawn up by the neighbours. Just then a neighbour came in to borrow the newspaper.

"Another commission from the old woman?" she said.

The militia officer laughed.

"You tell us," he said, "do you, or do you not, find the lion a nuisance?"

"Not a bit!" she said, flinging out her arms. "As if our Kinuli could be a nuisance!"

Then another one came in.

"We won't let them take our Kinuli away! We didn't bring her up, but we went through a lot while she was growing up."

Then we went in to Kinuli. The great yellow cat got lazily to her feet. She came up to me and rubbed her head affectionately against my knee.

The rest of the neighbours were waiting in the hall for the officer to come out. Everyone was indignant with the old woman, and Tolya's friend Yura, forgetting how Kinuli had once pulled his shorts off him, so that he had had to run back to his room naked, vowed that he would not let them take away Kinuli.

The officer pressed my hand warmly in farewell.

70

"We are perfectly satisfied, Comrade," he said. "Everything is quite clear now. You won't have any more trouble, and if anyone annoys you, ring me up."

We all stood a long time at the open door, calling after him :

"Thank you, officer! Thank you!"

And the next day I got a letter, saying:

"State District Sanitary Inspection, in consideration of the fact, now elucidated, that the lioness living in your flat is not dangerous, and is at present in delicate health, has rescinded its order for the transfer of the lioness to the Zoological Gardens within three days, and the animal may remain with you till its complete recovery, and till weather conditions are found suitable for its transfer."

Kinuli was allowed to go on living with us, and that was all we wanted.

BIRTHDAY

I was awakened early in the morning by a ring at the door. I leaped out of bed, threw on my dressing-gown and hurried to open the door. Who could it be? Why so early?

It was the postman. He smiled amiably and held out a letter to me. On the envelope was written in a careful, childish hand:

Kinuli Chaplin
Bolshaya Dmitrovka Street
Moscow

At first I could not understand. Neither the number of the house, nor of the flat was on the envelope. Very strange! And then I suddenly remembered—it was the 20th of April, Kinuli was a year old, and her young friends were hastening to wish their favourite many happy returns of the day. This put me into the best of spirits. I laughed, and the postman laughed. Before turning away he asked me to give Kinuli *his* birthday greetings, too, and kept looking back and nodding to me as he went down the stairs.

When I went into Vasya's room, Kinuli was still asleep. She always woke up early, when Vasya did, but as soon as he left for work, she went back to bed. Perry greeted me affectionately, but Kinuli was in no hurry to get up.

"Kinuli!" I cried. "Get up, lazybones! It's your birthday, you're a year old, and you lie sprawling there!"

Kinuli stretched lazily, and yawned. "Shall I get up, or not?" her drowsy, half-shut eyes seemed to be saying. But the moment Perry came up to me, Kinuli sprang up. She could not bear anyone else to be petted, and, jealously pushing the dog away, started rubbing against my legs.

There was a lot to be done that day. Things had to be bought to make a birthday dinner for Kinuli from her favourite dishes. And a big football must be bought. It was Tolya who had the idea of buying Kinuli a ball. He had been saving up to buy one for a long time.

By the evening everything was ready. The table was laid, Masha had fried rissoles, and Kinuli's presents lay on the sofa. Among them were—a new bowl, a clockwork motor-car, and three huge footballs, blown up so big that they looked ready to burst. One was from Tolya, the other two were sent us with birthday greetings by strangers.

The guests soon came.

That day Kinuli had dinner with us. She sat on the sofa eating her soup carefully out of her new bowl. The bowl stood on the table, but Kinuli was such a tidy eater that not a spot was made on the white

72

cloth. When she had finished, she put out her paw, and, knocking gently on the table, asked for another helping. But she was not given any more soup, for Masha had made her rissoles and a big omelette as well, in honour of the day. After dinner, Kinuli's birthday letters were read aloud. They were almost all from children, and began like this: "Dear Kinuli, we love you very much and send you best wishes for your birthday."

At first Kinuli listened attentively, but then she got tired of listening. There were so many letters, and besides there was no more omelette left. She jumped off the sofa and suddenly came face to face with the footballs. They were lovely new tan-coloured balls. She had long ago torn up her old one and now she pounced on them in a single bound, seizing them in her paws, and trying to hold them all. The balls rolled away, and Kinuli, a year-old lioness, oblivious to everything else in the world, ran after them like a kitten. It was impossible to watch her without laughing. The balls flew about the room, rolling under chairs, tables and the sofa. The very furniture seemed to have come to life. Everything in the room moved, even the bed rode on Kinuli's back to the other side of the room when the ball rolled under it.

Kinuli got so excited that it was impossible to pacify her. We tried to take away the balls, but Kinuli lay on them, clutching them between her paws, and refusing to give them up. It was Masha who found a way out of the difficulty. She called Perry and pretended she was going to take her for a walk. Kinuli abandoned the balls immediately and rushed after the dog. She did not like being left alone.

We always had a great deal of trouble in taking the dog out without Kinuli. As soon as Perry tried to go out of the room, Kinuli went after her, pushing her away from the door with her paw. We had to think up all sorts of tricks. I would try to distract Kinuli by petting her, Vasya stood by the door so as to shut it in time, and Masha picked up Perry and ran down the passage with her. But the abduction was not always successful. Sometimes Kinuli broke away, rushed after Masha, got Perry away from her, and went back to her room dragging the dog by the scruff of the neck. We called this "the abduction of Perry." Perry was quite used to such treatment, and allowed herself to be dragged back without offering the least resistance.

IN THE ZOO

The winter passed almost unnoticed, spring came, and then summer, and with summer the time for removing Kinuli to the Zoo. This was not because we were tired of her, or found her a nuisance. Quite the contrary. For the older she grew the more obedient and docile she became. She now had a much truer notion of the strength of her paws, the sharpness of her claws—each as long as a finger. She never hurt you if she happened to touch you with her paw while playing, and she never once so much as tore a stocking now. Nor did she spoil things any more. And Masha could leave the dishes on the table, even meat, and Kinuli touched nothing. In a word she behaved like a well-trained dog.

She had not changed towards Perry either. For the dog, Kinuli was still just a little kitten. Perry followed on Kinuli's heels, licked her muzzle clean after food as before, stood up for her, looked after her. And the lioness paid her back in the same coin. Never once did she eat up all her meat without leaving a bit for the dog. And so when Kinuli was being fed Perry would lie quietly at a little distance. Sometimes Kinuli would remember us, too. She would bring me or

Vasya a nasty, gnawed bone, and thrusting the messy thing right into our faces, invite us to have a bite.

We hated to part with her. But part we must. The militia would not allow us to keep a lioness in our flat any longer—she was a very big animal, and there were a lot of people about. Supposing she were to bite someone, one day!

And so they began to build a house for Kinuli in the Zoo, next to the young animals' territory. When the house was ready, a table and some chairs were put in it, and a small enclosure was railed off for Kinuli to play and romp in.

The day for her departure came. We all got up very early. It was decided to take Kinuli in a car, but nobody knew how she would like this, for she was a big lion now, and had not been in one for a long time. It was decided to make all preparations before the arrival of the car. A collar, specially made for the journey, had to be put on her, and the strength of the strap tested. And then something happened which none of us had foreseen. Before I could put the collar on her Kinuli gave a roar, knocked it out of my hand with her paw, and leaped aside. As it turned out, the collar had been smeared with tar, and the unfamiliar smell alarmed her. We tried all sorts of things. We rubbed the collar with meat and butter, but nothing was any good. Even when we put the collar on Perry, and got the dog to go up to Kinuli, Kinuli would not let her come near her. We had to send hurriedly to the chemist's for a wide bandage, which we folded in five breadths, to make a collar. Kinuli at once allowed us to put this on her.

The car came at ten o'clock. The driver drew up in the yard, and we went out with Kinuli. Poor puss! She was so upset that she did not even notice when we put the collar on her. Three of us held on to the leash—Vasya, Shura and I. Tolya went in front with Perry. If a single one of us stayed behind, Kinuli refused to go on.

In this way we went out of the flat and down the stairs, when suddenly Kinuli took fright and darted back. The strap broke under the strain, and the great yellow lioness rushed home as frightened as a kitten. It did not take her a minute to open the door, and by the time we arrived she was already under the table in her room.

At last we managed with the utmost difficulty to get her out and lure her into the waiting car. Vasya, Shura, little Tolya, Perry and I piled into the car, and tried to persuade Kinuli to get in. She walked round and round for a long time, mewing plaintively, before she could bring herself to do so. But once in, she got straight up on to the seat. She sat with her back paws weighing Vasya down, and her front paws on my lap, and lay quiet the whole way.

In the Zoo a run flooded with sunshine awaited Kinuli, and there were some early visitors, who had got wind that she was coming. When she found herself in a strange place, Kinuli lost her head. She crouched on the ground, hiding her great head under Perry and trembling violently.

I spent that night with her in the cage. All night Kinuli either strode restlessly up and down, trying to get the door open with her paw, or stopped abruptly to listen to the strange sounds of the Zoo at night.

In the morning I went home. Kinuli tried to get out after me, knocking her head again and again against the bars, and suddenly, as if she understood that she would not be able to get out, lay down, huddled up.

Kinuli would not move or eat for a long time. With unseeing eyes she stared into the distance through the bars, past trees, buildings, fences. Her eyes, always so lively and expressive, were now dull, more like the eyes of a dead than a living animal. This look in her eyes, so apathetic and indifferent, alarmed me more than anything else.

She did not even seem to recognize *me*. Occasionally, after long pleadings, she would take a bit of meat from my hand. Sometimes she would swallow it, but more often the meat hung from her fangs till it fell, and Kinuli did not even turn her head. She only began to come to herself after about ten days. She could hardly move on her feeble paws, but she began to show an interest in the animals and people around her. Our whole family went to see her every day. Kinuli rejoiced as never before when Vasya, Shura and Tolya came. She rubbed against their legs fondly, begging to be petted.

Early in the morning, before the Zoo was opened, I used to take her out for a walk. I took her without a collar. Since her arrival at the Zoo Kinuli had not allowed a collar to be put on her. So I had to take her without a leash. She walked beside me like a great docile dog. And how astonished the other animals were to see her! The deer followed her with terrified glances, ready to stampede. Leaping lightly from rock to rock, a flock of ibexes disappeared round the side of the hill, and the baby elephant, after first rushing at Kinuli, hid behind its house, as if alarmed by its own audacity. Kinuli passed by without paying the slightest attention to any of them. She took no notice of the shouts of the public, either.

There were always spectators in front of Kinuli's cage. They would wait patiently by the hour for the lioness to come out of her house. Many came every day to see how she was getting on.

I shall never forget three little girls who came running up to Kinuli's cage early one morning, as soon as the Zoo was open. The first, panting from her run, asked:

"How is Kinuli?"

And when she was told that Kinuli was getting better she turned to her companions, who were just running up, and shouted joyfully:

"Kinuli's getting better!"

The last time they had seen Kinuli she was ill and they had been so worried that they had dropped in before their exams to see her.

There were people who were worried about me too. If for some reason I was not in Kinuli's enclosure, they would ask the attendant what had happened. They wanted to know if I was not afraid of Kinuli, if she wouldn't kill me. I told them that if she were to do that she would die of grief herself afterwards.

For though Kinuli lived in a cage now, she had not changed towards me in the least. She was as affectionate and tame as ever. Just as before, she would lie down when told to, and let her coat be brushed and combed. I would tug her up by her paws, turn her over on her side and even pull her tail. Kinuli bore it all—anything to make me stay a little longer in her cage! Sometimes, if she was naughty, I would pretend to go. Then Kinuli would rush after me, catch at me with her paws, and refuse to let me go. Her claws were long and sharp, but she never hurt me with them. She would take bits of meat carefully from between my fingers, and when I left, looked after me for a long time, and at last raised her head and uttered the true lion's roar.

The summer passed, and the cold winter came. Kinuli and Perry were moved to winter quarters. Kinuli was now a full-grown lioness, and she was put into a cage next to other lions. There were always interested spectators in front of her cage. Everyone was astonished to see such a big lioness living with a dog.

Kinuli and Perry were great friends. When Kinuli was given meat she always left some for Perry. And while the dog ate, the lioness stood over her and would not allow the attendant to clean up till Perry had eaten her fill.

Once Perry fell ill. She was quite an old dog and had had pains in her legs for some time, and now she could not get up. Kinuli was terribly upset. Why didn't Perry get up? Why didn't she eat her meat? Kinuli took her own share to the dog, mewing and trying to lift her with her paw. But Perry did not get up. Then a doctor was called. The doctor wished to examine Perry, and the dog had to be taken out of the cage. But Kinuli refused to part with her friend—whenever anyone came for Perry she would roar and throw herself on the railings like a wild lioness. After great efforts she was lured into another cage, and only then could Perry be taken out.

When Kinuli saw that they had taken Perry away she began banging on the railings, trying to get out of the cage. She ate nothing that day, or the next. She grew dull, languid and cross, and would not let anyone come near her. She often roared, terrifying the other inhabitants of the Zoo.

Perry heard her too. She knew Kinuli's roar from all the other lion voices in the Zoo, and, pricking up her pointed ears, whined very softly.

Two months passed. Perry had grown well and strong, and could stand quite firmly on her legs again. It was time to put her back with Kinuli.

Kinuli saw Perry coming from a long way off. She cocked her ears and looked long and steadily at her. Oh, how glad they were to be together again! Kinuli rushed up to Perry, mewing, and rubbed her head against Perry so hard that we thought she would crush her. And the dog, quite forgetting her poor legs and her age, romped around the lioness like a puppy.

That day Kinuli and Perry ate well, and slept all night pressed against one another, and Kinuli's melancholy roar was not heard again.

PARTING

Then came June, 1941. War began.

The Zoo changed beyond recognition. Trenches intersected its smooth walks like deep wrinkles. The boards showing the way to the various animal houses now bore the brief inscription in black letters: "Bomb Shelter." In the town, alerts gave warning of the enemy's approach. The animals listened nervously to the wailing sirens, darting with terrified cries about their cages.

The lions were the most nervous of all, their loud roars blending with the hum of the first enemy aeroplanes to get through to Moscow.

On that memorable night of the first air-raid none of us went home. We all kept watch beside the animals, and put out the fires which started in several buildings. Fortunately these were not animal houses, or the wild beasts, breaking loose, might have done a great deal of harm. It became imperative to evacuate all the dangerous animals immediately.

Of the lions it was decided to leave only Kinuli, as the tamest and least dangerous, who, even if she got out of her cage, would not have touched anyone.

Despite the hard times, the youngsters of Moscow did not forget Kinuli. They enquired where she went during air-raids and advised having her taken to the Metro station. The animals were sent to other zoos, some to Stalingrad, some to Sverdlovsk. In the autumn I parted with Kinuli and went to Sverdlovsk, where I continued working in the Zoo. I spent all my spare time in the hospital, caring for the wounded, who soon discovered that I worked in the Zoo.

Some of the patients had even heard of Kinuli. They asked me to tell them about her. The moment I began doing something, I would be asked: "Tell us more about the lioness, nurse." The wounded from other wards came to ask about her. This even led to occasional arguments.

"You have your own nurses, let them tell you stories, leave ours alone!" the wounded in my ward would say.

Even the seriously wounded took an interest in Kinuli, and asked where she was, and how she was getting on.

Every letter from Moscow brought me news of Kinuli. They wrote me that Kinuli was quite well and that, though there were very few visitors to the Zoo, there was always somebody standing in front of her cage. Then I heard that Perry was ill, and later that she was dead, and now Kinuli was alone.

MEETING

Eighteen months later I was in Moscow again, and hastened to the Zoo. There was Kinuli's house. She was lying in a corner of her cage, eating meat. A few visitors were looking on.

I went up to the cage and joined them. A man next to me began telling me about Kinuli—how she had been brought up in a flat, and chased a thief on to the top of a cupboard, and a few other incidents from her life, but I did not listen very attentively.

I was standing quite close to Kinuli, but could not bring myself to call to her. It was not that I feared she would not recognize me. No, it was not that! It was nothing but jealous misgivings: supposing Kinuli won't leave her meat to come to me, supposing she doesn't come up to me at once, doesn't show me affection, as she used to!

So I stood in front of her cage and looked at the big yellow lioness, at the two familiar spots near her nose and called Kinuli in a whisper.

Kinuli heard me at once. She stopped eating, pricked up her ears and looked at me long and steadily. Then she got up, took a few uncertain steps in my direction and stopped.

Here I could not restrain myself any longer:

"Kinuli! Kinuli! Pussykins!"

Hardly had I time to get the words out and put my hands through the bars of her cage, when Kinuli rushed up to me, hitting herself so violently against the bars that blood trickled from her nose and mouth. But she took no notice of the pain, and rubbed lovingly against me.

I stayed with Kinuli for over an hour, but as I was leaving, one of the lion-house attendants caught me up in the office.

"Vera Vasilyevna, go to Kinuli," he begged. "She's bruised herself all over, and keeps roaring. I gave her some meat but she won't touch it, she keeps looking at the door."

I had to go back. Kinuli really would not eat. She was tearing up and down her cage, stopping every now and again, and banging herself against the railings with piteous roars. Visitors had gathered round her cage. They were all trying to comfort her, the man who had told me about Kinuli trying hardest of all.

The moment Kinuli saw me she rushed first to me and then to the meat, picking it up and trying to push it to me through the railings. I was longing to go into the cage and pet her, but could not do so without permission.

I was only allowed to go into Kinuli's cage a few days later, and then on condition that every precaution was taken. Kinuli was driven early in the morning into the outer cage. Prodding irons, rods, lassoes were held in readiness, and a great rubber hose was brought in and connected with the water pipe.

In a word, when, at the time appointed, I arrived, all preparations

6*

had been completed, and Kinuli was still tearing up and down her cage, roaring nervously.

As soon as she caught sight of me she gave a long-drawn affectionate mew and almost as soon as I opened the door of the cage, she rushed up to me.

I had the greatest trouble in keeping on my feet, so violent were Kinuli's demonstrations of affection.

And now nobody doubted any more that Kinuli would never forget me, and I was surer of this than anyone else.

THE WOLF'S NURSLING

IN A STRANGE CAGE

I N ONE CAGE lived a wolf, in the next an Alsatian sheep-dog. The cages were separated by iron bars, and both animals were in expectation of a litter. They had their babies almost simultaneously. Both mammas looked after their offspring conscientiously, when there suddenly occurred the incident I am going to relate.

One day, while the dog was gnawing at a bone contentedly, one of its puppies, the smallest and friskiest, crawled a little distance away. It crawled round and round till it got quite near the bars between the cages, just where some of them were slightly bent. Even this tiny opening was enough for the puppy to squeeze through and make its appearance in the wolf's cage.

The attendant saw this and tried to get hold of the pup. He picked up the metal club used for cleaning the cages and thrust it between the bars, drawing the pup towards him. All this time the mother wolf kept her eyes fixed on the adventurous stranger. Several times she seemed to be on the point of bounding up to it, but each time her fear of the club restrained her.

The pup was quite close to the front bars of the cage, when suddenly the mother wolf leaped up and seized it between her teeth. The attendant was alarmed. He thought the wolf would kill the puppy immediately, and began shouting and banging with the club to make the wolf drop it. But the wolf would not let go of the puppy. She took it over to a corner of the cage and placed it carefully among her cubs.

And so the puppy began to live with the wolf cubs.

A brisk little black creature, it contrasted sharply with its foster-brothers and sisters, and though considerably smaller than they were, developed much more quickly.

It always got first to the teats of its foster-mother, and was the first to hoist itself on to its feeble legs, the first to begin eating meat.

And when the wolf cubs grew up and began to play it showed itself to be the cleverest and most agile of them all.

It grew up quite wild. Like the wolf cubs it retreated into the corner of its cage when the attendant came in, silently baring its tiny fangs if anyone stretched out a hand to it.

APPROPRIATE NAME

The wolf cubs were two and a half months old. They hardly ever took milk from their mother now, for they could eat meat perfectly well. They were soon moved to the young animals' enclosure, where there were fox cubs, baby bears, two kids, some dingoes and Ussuri raccoons. And the puppy went there along with the wolf cubs.

The attendant took the wolf cubs out of their basket one by one by the scruff of their necks, examined each carefully, and gave it a name. All their distinguishing marks were entered in a notebook and only then the wolf cubs were let out into the run. The cubs dangled from her hands—heavy-headed and resigned, their mouths half-open, their tails tucked between their legs. When set at liberty they lay for some time on the ground as if dead, and then shambled off to a secluded corner.

The puppy behaved quite differently. When the attendant picked it up it gave a piercing yelp, twisting and turning, and snapping at her hand. She was so astonished that she dropped it. She was going to pick it up again, when it escaped and tore off across the enclosure.

The attendant looked after the puppy, wiped the blood from her hand, and wrote under the heading "Name" in her notebook: Kusaka.* This name suited the puppy perfectly. At first the attendants tried to tame the little savage, but Kusaka stubbornly avoided human beings and snapped so viciously at anyone who tried to stroke her that she was soon left in peace.

In her romps with the other animals Kusaka showed more agility and ingenuity every day.

* From the verb *kusat*—to bite.—*Tr.*

She could turn in full gallop and fall upon her pursuer, or wriggle out of the powerful embrace of a half-grown bear cub, and jump at it from all sides, so that the bear, its head swimming, had to escape up a tree. Kusaka's romps often turned into real hunting. Sometimes she would chase the other animals so wildly that the attendant would have to interfere.

The attendants did not like Kusaka—because of her they dared not leave the enclosure for a moment. They always had to be on the look-out to see that she did not hurt any of the others. The kids had to be removed from the enclosure, for Kusaka all but killed them. The tiresome dog was borne with for three months, but in the autumn, after she had killed two fox cubs and seriously wounded a bear cub, it was decided to get rid of her.

In spite of all this I liked Kusaka. She was not particularly handsome, but I liked her agility and liveliness. Her colouring was very unusual—the body black, the paws and cheeks yellowish. This made her face very expressive. It changed from anger to delight very rapidly. When she laughed she stretched her mouth so wide that her yellow cheeks reached almost up to her ears, and her eyes slanted and sparkled with mirth. And I liked her for her indomitable spirit.

So when I heard Kusaka was to be got rid of, I asked for her. I cannot say that my family were particularly pleased. They had heard a lot about Kusaka and were not very anxious to have her in their midst.

When I went for Kusaka she was running about the enclosure. It would have been very hard to catch her there and so it was decided to lure her into the cage. We opened the door of the cage and threw a bit of meat into it. Quite unsuspicious, Kusaka went in at once. I got in after her and shut the door quickly. Seeing a stranger so near, Kusaka began tearing about the cage in terror, then, just as quickly, her behaviour changed. She bristled up, gathered herself into a bunch, and retreated slowly into a corner, baring her teeth. I thought I would see what a show of affection would do, but at my first attempt her eyes became so vicious that I had to give up the idea at once. Then I took up a strap and tried to get the loop over her head. I managed to do this at the very first attempt, but failed to draw it tight in time. Kusaka wriggled out of it very cleverly and rushed at me. She attacked me again and again, silently gnashing her teeth, like a wolf, and trying with obstinate rage to get at my face. But at last I put the loop over her head. And how furious she was when she felt the strap round her neck! She made frantic efforts to free herself, squealing madly, and snapping at everything that came her way; suddenly she began biting at her own side, her paw, tearing at herself as if at an enemy. Kusaka's gleaming black fur was stained with blood, and she rolled on the ground, biting at herself again and again.

With a supreme effort I got hold of her by the scruff of the neck and pressed her to the ground. Then I quickly took out another strap and bound her muzzle and paws with it. Now she lay quite helpless, but her eyes blazed with such ferocity that I turned away involuntarily. And yet, for all this, I liked the wolf's nursling.

The zoological technician and I took Kusaka out of the cage, put her in a car and drove off with her. At that time I was living in a small cottage on the New Territory of the Zoo. I placed a kennel for Kusaka not far away, beside a big tree. Putting a strong, wide collar round her neck, I fastened it to a long chain, and then, freeing her muzzle and paws, moved away.

Kusaka lay motionless for some time, then suddenly sprang up and bounded forward with such violence that the chain pulled her up short, and she was thrown backwards. She lunged forward again, trying to break away and whining, but soon exhausted herself, and slunk into the kennel, where she stayed all day, refusing food. All night we could hear her tugging and whining, and for a long time she gave wolf-like howls. When I went out the next morning Kusaka retreated into the kennel. Her food was untouched and some bloody froth on the ground bore witness to the vain attempts she had made to bite through her chain.

A WILD BEAST BECOMES A DOG

It took Kusaka a long time to get used to us.

She lay for days in her kennel, and would not touch her food while any of us were about. She only ate when we went away. Looking round suspiciously she would go up to the bowl, eat the food in it, and return to her place. At night she howled, she never barked. I forbade anyone to go near her, in case she bit them—especially the children. I wondered very much when the dog would show through the wolfish upbringing. I had to wait a long time, but in the end it did. It began when Kusaka was no longer indifferent to my leaving her. When she saw me getting ready to go, she would prick up her ears, stick her head out of the kennel, and at last come out, following me attentively with her eyes. Sometimes I would hide behind the corner of the house for a little time and come suddenly back. Kusaka would tuck in her tail with an embarrassed air and turn away slowly. But she never paid the slightest attention to my children, Tolya and Lyuda, and did not even seem to know them from other children.

But this was not really so, and once she showed that she did know them.

Some children were passing by our house. One of them carried a ball, the other knocked it out of his hands in play. The ball bounced

on to the ground and rolled into Kusaka's kennel. The children tried to get it out with a stick, but Kusaka snatched the stick so furiously from their hands that they had to give up the attempt. They asked me to get them their ball. I could only have done this by dragging Kusaka out by the chain, and I did not want to shake the confidence she was beginning to place in me. I persuaded the children to come the next day for their ball and was just going away when I caught sight of Lyuda. She went boldly up to Kusaka with the simplicity and fear-lessness of a child. I was going to shout to her, to run to her, but it was too late. Lyuda was already bending over the ball, the slender neck of the five-year-old child was on a level with the jaws of the ferocious dog. I stood as if hypnotized, not daring to move. I knew that, at the slightest sound or movement, Kusaka might have fallen upon Lyuda. Now Lyuda was stretching her hands out towards the ball.... Kusaka moved a little to the side.... Lyuda picked up the ball ... went away holding it.... I snatched her up, kissing her over and over again. And I felt I must give Kusaka something nice for not touching the child. I ran into the house and fished a piece of meat out of the soup, and held it out to Kusaka. But she would not let me go beyond a certain point, showing her teeth and snarling warningly.. I put down the meat and went away.

From that day I no longer forbade the children to go to Kusaka, only telling them not to go *too* near. But Tolya and Lyuda disobeyed me. They used my permission in a very broad sense. Their favourite playground was next to Kusaka. Lyuda made mud pies and castles. Kusaka obviously took a great interest in this. She would come out of her kennel, and sit and watch the children from a distance.

Kusaka now knew our whole family. Every day she allowed me to come a little nearer. Sometimes she even tried to come to me herself, but the chain held her back. She was still frightened by the slightest tug or movement. Noticing this I decided to let Kusaka off the chain. Everybody tried to dissuade me, assuring me she would run away. But something told me she would not. I took a sharp knife, fixed it to a stick, and carefully cut the collar. The collar and chain fell heavily to the ground.

Kusaka was free. She could go where she liked. She could run away altoge.her, there was nothing to keep her. But Kusaka did not run away. Neither on that day nor the next few days. Something held her back—something that was stronger than a chain.

Every morning when I went to work she followed me to the gate. Every evening she ran to meet me. She no longer slept in her kennel, but spent the night in a deep hole under the porch which she had dug with her paws. She did not howl so much, and one day we heard her bark. It was in the night. Kusaka loved to roam over the deserted Zoo territory at night, and once she came up against a watchman. With her tail tucked in, her pointed nose, upright ears and her whole demeanour, she looked exactly like a wolf. And, like a wolf, on catching sight of a man, she silently took cover of the dark. The watchman, taking her for a wild beast that had escaped from its cage, followed her.

Kusaka retreated timidly from him till she got up to our house. Seeing a light in the window, the watchman went up to it, and then— oh, then Kusaka behaved quite unlike a wolf! Turning swiftly she threw herself on the man. That was the time we heard her first bark— sharp broken sounds, interrupted by the snapping of her teeth. At first I could not believe my ears, but when cries for help were added to the barking I hastened out of the house.

Poor watchman! He found it hard to beat off Kusaka, who leaped round and round him, trying to get at his ankles.

I expected to have trouble in driving her away. But it was quite easy. The moment I called her by her name, she stopped attacking the man, went obediently away from him and allowed him to go.

Kusaka took a great interest in our daily life. If we chanced to leave the door open she would come up, sit in the doorway and follow all our movements with her eyes. When the door was shut at night, she would often put her front paws on the window-sill and peer into the lighted room.

But it was a long time before Kusaka allowed herself to be stroked. This happened after I had been away from home several days. I stayed away on purpose to see how Kusaka would take my absence. Tolya came and told me all she did and how she behaved. He said Kusaka always ran to the entrance of the Zoo at the time I usually came back from work, looking into the street for a long time, searching for me among the passers-by, and that she seemed unhappy and had no appetite. I came back in the day-time when Kusaka was not expecting me. She was lying beside the house, but the moment she saw me she rushed up to me. I stretched out my hand and Kusaka did not leap back as she used to. She thrust her nose into my hand and stood still, wagging her tail clumsily. I took advantage of her trustfulness to put my hand cautiously on her head, and stroke her. At first gently, then more and more boldly, I stroked her black satiny head, which I had been longing to touch for such a long time. Kusaka stood perfectly still when I touched her, as if frozen to the spot, and then slipped from beneath my hand, and began fawning on me just like a dog. She jumped up to my chest, wagged her tail, licked my hands and face. From a suspicious wild beast she had become a dog, the faithful friend of man.

It would be hard to imagine a dog more devoted than Kusaka. I cannot say she was particularly brave. She still had a great deal of the shyness and cautiousness of the wild animal in her. But whenever it seemed to her that the children or I were in danger she would fly boldly to our defence.

One day I went to the storehouse. It was on the New Territory, not far from our cottage, but Kusaka had never been there, for the five huge dogs which guarded the storehouse were her sworn enemies. She accompanied me up to the gate and waited outside. But hardly had I entered the yard when the dogs attacked me. Seeing me in danger Kusaka flung herself into the uneven battle. The five huge fierce dogs had her down in a moment. It was hard to make out anything in the writhing, growling mass. With enormous difficulty I managed, aided by the storehouse keeper, to pull off one of the dogs. We could do nothing with the rest. Every time they were pulled off they broke away and flew at Kusaka again. I thought they would kill her, but she fought like a wild beast.

The dogs attacked her from all directions, but she was a match for them.

The first to give up the battle was a young dog, and two of the others followed suit. Only one—the fiercest of all—a battle-scarred dog by the name of Barsuk—kept up the fight. Kusaka was much smaller and younger than Barsuk. But she had no intention of yielding to a foe so much stronger than herself. She fell upon Barsuk without the slightest attempt at retreating, and bit him on the muzzle. Barsuk was infuriated. He would certainly have killed Kusaka, but for the blood pouring from the many bites on his nose. He seized Kusaka by the throat again and again, throwing her on the ground, but each time, half-choked by his own blood, he let go. And Kusaka, almost suffocated, swaying with exhaustion, went for him again and again, biting at his muzzle.

Barsuk, who had never before met his equal in battle, gave in, terrified by the resolution and grip of this extraordinary dog, so unlike any he had ever seen before. And Kusaka! Kusaka could hardly crawl up to me, and lay down at my feet immediately. There did not seem to be a sound spot on her body. I tried to pick her up but she was too badly hurt for that. Then I cautiously helped her to her feet and led her home, gently supporting her.

Kusaka was ill for a long time, but the memory of this did not prevent her from defending Tolya just as energetically, when another occasion arose.

When Kusaka was a year old she was registered in the service-dog club. At that time all Alsatians had to be registered, and though Kusaka was the nursling of a wolf, she was an Alsatian and therefore came under the regulations.

Kusaka was examined and found unsuitable for training, there was too much of the wild beast still left in her. All this was entered on a card, and I was given a paper certifying that while her puppies might be demanded, she was not liable to mobilization. Unfortunately, however, I lost this certificate. And so when they came to fetch her I was unable to prove that Kusaka was no good for training purposes and that she could not even walk on a leash.

"We've trained more difficult dogs," they answered confidently.

Kusaka stood quiet while I buckled a stout leash to her collar, but the moment a stranger took hold of the end she gave signs of nervous-ness. And when they tried to take her with them, Kusaka showed the stuff she was made of. First she leaped at the man holding the leash. But these were experienced men, and they soon subdued her wild disposition. Then Kusaka tried to break away. Alternately throwing herself from side to side, and hurling herself on the ground, she flatly refused to go with them. They dragged her to the street somehow or other, but once there Kusaka began yelping and trying to break away. A crowd gathered. Everyone pitied the dog, and when the men again dragged her after them, Kusaka suddenly wriggled out of the collar and galloped off home.

Naturally the people who had come for her were disgusted. It would have been practically impossible to catch her on the huge territory. But they came for her again that same evening. This time they had a dog with them, specially brought to help catch Kusaka. Kusaka was lying in her kennel. One of the men quickly closed the opening of the kennel and the other, putting on thick mitts, lifted the lid of the kennel and boldly thrust his hands inside the opening. It was only a little opening, but it was enough for Kusaka—after all she had been brought up by a wolf. Hardly had the man bent over the lifted roof, when Kusaka leaped out of the opening, knocking the roof off with a single, powerful blow, so that it struck the man in the face with such force that the blood came. Kusaka disappeared behind a turning before he could recover his senses.

Their dog rushed after her, but came back very soon, bitten all over by the truant.

Furious at their failure, the men vowed they would not go back without Kusaka. They had never come up against such a dog before, and they determined to outwit her at all costs. They tied up their own dog, hung a noose in front of Kusaka's kennel, and hid behind the house. They had to wait a long time. It had struck midnight and they were still there, waiting for the dog. I came out several times myself to look for Kusaka, but she was nowhere to be seen. I began to be afraid she had run away. But the next morning, when the men, stiff with cold, and vexed at their failure, had gone, Kusaka came out from under the house, stretching luxuriously, just behind the place where the men had lain in ambush.

But a few days later they did take her. She was chained up and could not get away this time. They bound her up and took her away in a car. We all missed Kusaka, especially Tolya and Lyuda. And when I went to find out where she was, I was told they had not been able to take her to the kennels. In the train she had gnawed through her leash, leaped out of the van, and run away. They were sorry she was lost and added that if she turned up they would not take her again.

Then I started looking for her. I went to the station near which Kusaka had escaped and enquired among the inhabitants. But no one had seen a small black Alsatian, no one could tell me anything about her.

We had made up our minds that Kusaka was lost, when quite unexpectedly she came back, emaciated, filthy, with tattered fragments of strap on her collar. Where she had come from, how many miles she had traversed, and how she had found her home, we never knew, but no one came for her again and Kusaka remained with us. At night she kept watch, and in the day-time she slept calmly in her kennel. And so Kusaka, the wolf's nursling, found a place in life.

BABY

THE CLEVEREST OF ALL

OR A LONG TIME my work at the Zoo was with lions and tigers,
but one day I was transferred to work in the ape house.
I did not want to go there at all. I knew nothing about monkeys,
and I did not care for them. I stood in front of a cage of rhesus monkeys; there was a whole flock of them—about forty—running about.
I looked at them, thinking: "How shall I ever learn to know them
apart? They're so alike! The same eyes, tiny faces, hands—they
even seem to be all the same size!" But that was only at first; when
I got used to them I saw that though they were all the same breed,
they were not really like one another. Vovka had a head so smooth

it looked as if the fur had been combed back, while Bobrik's fur stood out all round, like a golliwog.

The most individual of them all was Baby. She was the smallest, and that was how she got her name. She had a tiny pointed face and was very lively and agile. When I went into the cage all the monkeys would scatter, but Baby would only move a very little way off and stare at the sieve in which I brought them fruit.

I made up my mind to tame Baby. But it was no easy matter.

For a long time the little coward did not venture to come to me, and ran away the moment I put out my hand. But I sat patiently in the cage for hours at a time, every now and then throwing her the daintiest titbits.

Gradually Baby began to get used to me. She no longer ran away when I came up to her and once actually plucked up enough courage to snatch at a biscuit I was offering to another monkey. Once she even tried to feel in my pocket, but ran away as soon as she stretched out her hand, startled by her own audacity. From that time I always put something sweet in my pocket. And I did it so that Baby could see. I discovered that she was a real sweet-tooth.

Baby watched intently when I put a pear or a lump of sugar in my pocket, puckering her little mouth and uttering plaintive cries. And at last she made up her mind to put her hand into my pocket. So as not to frighten the little thief I turned away, pretending to notice nothing. Baby quickly snatched a lump of sugar out of my pocket and darted off, sitting down not too near, so as to be out of harm's way, and glancing round furtively.

After this her shyness vanished completely. The moment I entered the cage she would jump on to my shoulder and make a thorough search. Her thin quick little hands went deftly through my pockets. Keys, money, handkerchief—Baby grabbed them all. Once she even got hold of a mirror, and climbed up to the roof of the cage to examine it. She turned it round and round, gazing at it, unable to understand where that other monkey had gone to. She tried to catch her reflection in all sorts of ways, peeping behind the mirror, grabbing at the reflection, even biting the glass. This alarmed me. Baby might break the glass and cut herself. I tried to take the mirror away from her, but this was not so easy. She ran all over the cage with it, and refused to give it up. I had to call Auntie Polya to my aid.

Auntie Polya had been looking after monkeys for a long time and they obeyed her. She came into the cage and threatened Baby with the broom. Baby knew and feared the broom, and immediately dropped the mirror.

PUNISHMENT FOR GREED

Like all monkeys Baby was very greedy. She was no longer afraid of me and when I went into the cage would pinch my arms if I gave food to another monkey. And my arms were often black and blue, for Baby could pinch very painfully. She was not even afraid of Grishka.

Grishka was a monkey too. But he was the leader. Many monkeys live in flocks in a wild state. The biggest and strongest monkey makes itself their leader, and protects the flock from danger. The monkeys obey and fear their leader. And in the cage, too, Grishka was obeyed and feared. When the monkeys were fed, not one of them dared to take a bit before he had eaten. They all waited for him to finish his meal. Grishka would choose the best bits at his leisure, going back to his favourite perch, with slow dignity, when he had eaten his fill. Only then, casting furtive glances at him, would the rest of the monkeys come up to the food. They would hastily stuff as much as they could into their cheek-pouches, and hurry back to their places. Grishka kept them all in a state of terror. *He* could hit or bite the monkeys as much as he liked but he allowed no fighting among the rest. And woe to anyone who attempted to hurt one of *his* monkeys! Whoever the foe might be, Grishka would rush to the defence. If Grishka felt cold he would gather the monkeys around him and make them warm him or search him for fleas.

Baby was the only one who dared to disobey Grishka. She never searched him for fleas or warmed him, as the other monkeys did. Quick and agile, she always managed to escape danger, or, feeling that she had a protector in me, would carry off food right under his nose. Stuffing her cheeks with nuts and apples, she would shuffle away clumsily, to eat in peace.

Grishka bore this for a long time. But once when Baby, having as usual grabbed a lot of food, was slowly climbing upwards, Grishka rushed at her. Baby, taken by surprise, dropped some of the food. Squealing, she tried to escape, but it was too late. Grishka held her firmly by the tail, hitting, biting and scratching her. Auntie Polya and I yelled at him and threatened him with the broom, Baby clung to the bars with her hands and feet and tried to get away—but in vain. Grishka dragged her right up to the roof of the cage, and took everything away from her—even a lump of sugar she had hidden in her cheek.

That is how Baby was punished for her greediness.

RUBBER FRIEND

Someone threw a sweet into the monkey cage. It was a coloured sweet wrapped up in paper. Baby ate it and it made her ill. She sat for days on her perch, looking very sad, all huddled up as if she

were cold. Her sides fell in, and her fur, always so gleaming, was
dull and shaggy.

Nobody jumped on to my shoulder now, or pinched my arms and
rifled my pockets.

The doctor was sent for. He examined the patient carefully and
prescribed castor oil and a hot-water bottle on her tummy.

Baby had to be given the castor oil by force, and she made still
more fuss about the hot-water bottle. Four times we tried to tie it to
her tummy and four times Baby shook it off.

Then we resorted to cunning.

Baby was put into a cage so small that she could hardly fit into
it, and a rubber hot-water bottle was placed on the floor. Oh, how

frightened Baby was! It lay there, so strange, so terrible, like a jelly-fish.

In her terror Baby huddled up in a corner of the cage, gazing at the bottle with horror in her eyes. She sat there motionless for hours. During that time we changed the water in the bottle several times, but Baby was too frightened even to stir. Then cautiously, never taking her eyes off the bottle, she drew nearer and touched it softly. The bottle was pleasantly warm and did not bite. Then, becoming bolder, she pressed up to it with the whole of her tiny, skinny body, holding it tight in her arms, and at last fell asleep.

From that day Baby could not be separated from the hot-water bottle. Holding it over her tummy, she moved with it from place to place, and even searched it for fleas. Of course there weren't any fleas, but searching for fleas is with a monkey the surest sign of good will. And how difficult it was to take the bottle away from Baby after she had recovered! She could not bear to be parted from her rubber friend, pressing it to her chest and crying as if her own child were being taken away from her.

For a whole month after Baby was back with her friends, if anyone passed by with a hot-water bottle, she would spring to the bars, protrude her lips and utter plaintive cries.

USELESS CUNNING

A monkey had to be sent to another Zoo. The train would leave in the evening. The choice fell on Baby. She was the tamest of all the monkeys and it would be easier to catch her than any of the others. At least that was what we thought—in reality it turned out quite otherwise. Hardly had the zoological technician entered the cage when all the monkeys were up at the top in a flash. They knew the Zoo technician very well, for he often had to catch a monkey. It was enough for him to appear in the distance for such a din to be raised that everyone knew at once who was coming.

Seeing that it would not be so easy to catch Baby, the Zoo technician resorted to a ruse. He put on Auntie Polya's blouse and skirt, put a shawl over his head and even changed his gait so that the monkeys should not know who it was coming into the cage. The monkeys stared at him in perplexity—it looked like Auntie Polya, and yet it was not her. They circled round him without venturing nearer. He threw a pear to this one, an apple to another, and crept closer and closer to Baby. He held out an apple to her.

I watched with a sinking heart: "He'll catch my Baby, he's sure to catch her." But I saw that Baby was not so simple as all that. She stretched out her hand for the apple, but glanced very suspiciously at the Zoo technician's feet. I looked down too, and saw his great boots showing under Auntie Polya's skirt. Baby had seen them too.

The boots came nearer and nearer, and Baby backed farther and farther away from them, looking at the boots all the time, and suddenly she gave a squeal. In a moment all the monkeys were at the top of the cage.

Then Grishka the leader growled out "Kra," and they all fell upon the man as if at a word of command. In a moment the shawl was torn off, Auntie Polya's skirt and new blouse were in rags. The Zoo technician tried to defend himself and shake them off, but forty pairs of agile monkey hands seized and tore at his clothes, pinched his face.

Auntie Polya came running up to see what the noise was about, and rushed to the assistance of the technician. But it proved no easy matter to rescue him from the infuriated monkeys, who refused to give up their victim. With the utmost difficulty, shielding his face and head with his hands, torn and scratched, the technician at last got out of the cage.

The monkeys were so excited that they could not calm down for a long time and kept making threatening gestures in his direction, and uttering loud cries.

This is how the cunning of the Zoo technician was defeated, and Baby stayed in the Zoo.

ESCAPE

When the warm sunny days came the monkeys were transferred from their winter house to a large, spacious open-air cage.

They ran about it all day, chasing one another, jumping from trapeze to trapeze like acrobats, walking along taught ropes, climbing up smooth poles.

Baby was the only one who did not romp. We were quite surprised —usually so playful, she would now sit for hours near the bars, looking out at some trees which grew near by. Sometimes the wind bent a branch a little nearer and then Baby would thrust her hand through the bars and try to get hold of it. Sitting back again she would gaze for hours at the closed door. And one day, when Auntie Polya opened the door a little wider than usual to get into the cage, Baby bounded past the attendant, and before Auntie Polya knew what was happening, she was at the very top of a tree. Auntie Polya tried in vain to get her back by calling to her and holding out the choicest titbits.

Auntie Polya's tears and entreaties were of no avail. The little runaway did not so much as turn her head, and when one of the managers and an attendant came to the assistance of Auntie Polya,

Baby jumped agilely on to another tree, leaped over a fence and rapidly disappeared from view.

A few minutes later messages began coming over all the Zoo telephones.

"Hullo! Has a monkey escaped from the Zoo? It's in Presnya Street!"

"Militia speaking. Is that your monkey last seen in the direction of Tishinskaya Street?"

Every time the manager put down the receiver fresh calls came in —from Georgiyevsky Square, from Bolshaya Gruzinskaya, from Kurbatovsky Street. Calls came from every street in which Baby appeared.

Auntie Polya and I rushed off to look for her. When we got to Kurbatovsky Street we saw a crowd in front of a house, and Baby skipping desperately about on the second storey window ledge.

Suddenly she jumped through an open window, knocking over some flowerpots.

Auntie Polya and I dashed into the house in a great hurry. We ran up the stairs and suddenly a woman burst out of one of the rooms. Guessing at once where our Baby was, we went into the room and saw the terrified monkey leaping from corner to corner. At last, after enormous efforts, we caught her.

We wrapped Baby up in a smock to prevent her escaping on the way home and hurried back with her to the Zoo.

Baby was put back into the cage. How glad the others were to see the truant back! They surrounded her, fondling her and chattering in their monkey language, and Baby sat on a perch, nibbling at an immense apple, given her by Auntie Polya.

FOMKA THE POLAR BEAR

FOUR-LEGGED PASSENGER

FOMKA ARRIVED in Moscow not by train or by steamer, but by aeroplane. He came straight from Kotelny Island to Moscow. Honoured aviator Ilya Pavlovich Mazuruk steered the plane. It was to him that the inhabitants of Kotelny had given this present, and the crew of the aeroplane decided to take it to Moscow.

Fomka—that was the cub's name—was put on the aeroplane in a crate. The crate was big and strong, and one side was left open and covered with wire netting. At first Fomka sat very still. But as soon as the plane took off he clutched at the netting, trying to tear it with his teeth and claws, and howling so loudly that not even the noise of the engines could drown his cries.

Nobody could quieten the little howler. Seal-meat, cod-liver oil and other bear dainties were put into the crate, but the cub only went on howling himself hoarse. Then it was decided to let him out, and his cage was opened.

Fomka came cautiously out of his cage as if danger lurked everywhere. Glancing suspiciously from side to side, he went all round the cabin, sniffed at everything, inspected everything, and at last climbed on to a big leather armchair and began gazing with curiosity out of the window. The leather armchair became his favourite place. Fomka slept, ate and spent almost all his time there. He was let out every time the plane landed. He soon learned to know when it was beginning to land, and would jump off the chair and go and sit beside the door. And how eagerly he jumped out when the door was opened! He tumbled head over heels down the steep ladder to the ground, and then his time for playing came. He rolled over and over on the grass, turned on his back and on his stomach, caught one of his hind feet with his front paws, held it tightly and wrestled with himself.

In his excitement he never even noticed the people who gathered round him. But however absorbed he was in his game, the moment anyone called out: "To the plane!" or the propeller roared, Fomka stopped playing and rushed back with all the fleetness of a bear.

He clambered up the ladder so funnily and awkwardly, was in such a hurry to be the first in the cabin, that you might have thought he was afraid of being left behind. And this is how Fomka, the polar bear, came to Moscow.

Ilya Pavlovich Mazuruk decided to keep Fomka in his flat for a while. But this turned out to be impossible. Imagine a polar bear with his warm fur coat, so warm that it was nothing but a pleasure for him to bathe on the most freezing day! And this bear lives, not in the Far North, amidst the wide spaces of eternal ice, but in the very middle of Moscow, in the steam-heated rooms of a town flat.

Fomka was so hot he didn't know what to do. His one salvation was the bath-room. The bath was filled to the brim for him. He would get into it, roll about, dive, splash the water with his paws.

The walls of the room were always splashed after the bear's bath, and there were puddles on the floor.

After his bath Fomka would get out and slide over the polished floor as if it were ice and get, dripping wet, on to the sofa or into bed. There was no managing him. Ilya Pavlovich bore it as long as he could, but at last he could stand it no longer. He telephoned to the Zoo and begged them to take the cub away. "Do come! Help me! Polar bears don't know how to behave in rooms."

They sent me to fetch Fomka.

When I arrived Fomka was asleep on the floor in the middle of the big study. His four paws pointed in all four directions, and he looked like a little rug.

Fomka slept so soundly that he did not even wake when I picked him up.

He only woke up out in the street, from the cry of an old woman: "Good heavens! Is that a bear she's carrying?"

Fomka roared, struggled out of my arms and scampered up to a motor-car drawn up beside the kerb, which he probably took for the aeroplane. He seized the handle and tugged at it, to the terror of the passengers. Seeing a white bear trying to get into their car they jumped out, shouting loudly, through the other door. This frightened Fomka still more. How he roared! And how he tugged at the handle! The door gave under his weight and opened, and before I knew where

I was Fomka was inside, on the seat. He calmed down at once, but the owners of the car shouted still louder, scolding and demanding that the bear should be turned out. This was all very well—but Fomka did not want to get out. I pulled him and he stuck where he was, growling and scratching.

A militiaman came up to see what the noise was about. He listened to all we had to say and unexpectedly declared:

"Instead of raising a din in the street, comrades, you'd better help take the animal to the Zoo."

The militiaman's words had their effect. The owners of the car calmed down and politely offered me their car, consenting to go in the Zoo car themselves. We had to change not only cars, but drivers, too, their driver refusing point-blank to drive a car with a bear in it.

Fomka sat quiet the whole way, gazing attentively out of the window, and the passers-by halted, looking after us and wondering how a polar bear had got into a motor-car.

We arrived at the Zoo without mishap. Fomka, it is true, had no desire to get out of the car, but this time the Zoo technician came to our aid. Choosing a convenient moment, he seized Fomka by the scruff of the neck, and before the bear had time to recover from the shock it was safely in the cage.

CURIOUS DISEASE

Fomka was not in the least disturbed to find himself in a new place. He made the round of the cage, sniffed at it, got into the sleeping place at the back and went straight to sleep. Meanwhile Katya, the attendant of the baby animals, carefully prepared a meal for him. We had never before had a polar bear cub on our territory and we all wanted him to have something nice.

At last it was agreed to make a milk gruel and give Fomka some seal fat, and Katya decided to add a carrot and an apple as her personal contribution.

When everything was ready Fomka woke up. You should have seen the pride with which we offered him his first dinner. In front, carrying the gruel, went Lipa, a student doing her practice at the Zoo, after her came Katya with the carrot and apple, looking very grand and important, and I came last with the seal fat, which smelled so horrible that I had to hold my nose with my free hand.

The first to go into the cage was Lipa. Almost as soon as she had put down the bowl of gruel, Fomka overturned it, sniffed at it, and shambled up to Katya. Katya placed the carrot and apple in front of him and produced a biscuit from her pocket. Fomka took no notice of these dainties, either. Now he was standing at the bars looking greedily at me. I opened the door and the seal fat slithered down to the feet of the cub like a great jelly-fish. We thought Fomka would surely eat now. But our hopes were disappointed. The cub grabbed the seal fat greedily, but let it go instantly. Then we brought a little of everything that had been prepared for the other animals and put it in front of Fomka.

But this was not acceptable either. Fomka sniffed at everything, turned it all over, but ate nothing. At first we thought he simply wasn't hungry, but when, that evening, he bawled at the top of his voice from hunger, and still refused all food, we sent for the doctor. When the doctor came he wanted to examine the cub, but Fomka raised such a din and was so violent that the doctor was afraid to go into his cage, and anyhow Fomka did not look at all like an invalid. Everyone was puzzled by his behaviour, and it was decided to wait and see what the next day would bring.

Fomka roared and thrashed about all night, and when morning came still refused to eat. I had to go back to Mazuruk. Perhaps Fomka would not eat because he missed his master.

Ilya Pavlovich received me in the most friendly manner. He asked so many questions about his nursling that I could hardly bear to disappoint him immediately. But at last I had to tell him that Fomka would not eat. He heard me out and suddenly burst out laughing. Just then the telephone bell rang. Ilya Pavlovich picked up the receiver—

it was an urgent call for him. Promising to look in at the Zoo later, he went away.

Ilya Pavlovich kept his word. He came that same evening with a small suitcase in his hand and went straight up to Fomka's cage. We had no idea what was in the suitcase. Ilya Pavlovich placed it beside him and said he would soon cure Fomka. Then he took a big clasp-knife out of his pocket. We were greatly surprised and could not help asking what the knife was for, and if we hadn't better send for a doctor.

But Ilya Pavlovich only chuckled mysteriously, opened the suit-case and took out of it a tin on which was written: "Condensed Milk." He opened it with the knife and handed it to Fomka. Fomka grabbed it eagerly with his front paws and lapped up the milk with his long red tongue, after which he licked the can all over till it shone like silver.

While Fomka was eating, Ilya Pavlovich explained to us the secret of Fomka's "illness." The cub had been fed with nothing but con-densed milk in the aeroplane, and had grown so accustomed to it that he would take no other food.

It cost us a lot of trouble to wean Fomka from this delicacy. He was very naughty, obstinately refusing all other food, and we had to add condensed milk to everything before he would eat it. By adding it to his porridge, to soup and even to cod-liver oil, we gradually cured him of his "illness," and got him on to the proper diet for a polar bear.

FOMKA MAKES FRIENDS

We soon let Fomka go to the young animals' enclosure. At first we kept him alone, but Fomka would not play by himself. He strode up and down, whining plaintively from loneliness. Then we decided to introduce him to the other baby animals. We let fox cubs, bear cubs, wolf cubs and baby raccoons on to the run. When they were all playing together, we let Fomka go to them.

Fomka came out of his cage as if he did not see anyone, but by the way he wheezed and drooped his head, and by the gleam in his tiny eyes, we could tell that he saw everything and everyone.

And the other cubs saw him at once, but each of them reacted in its own way—the wolf cubs tucked in their tails, moving aside with cautious glances, the fur of the raccoons bristled up till they looked like great balls, the badgers scattered in all directions and were hidden from view in a moment. But the brown bears were frightened most of all. They stood up on their hind legs all together, blinking and gazing in utter amazement at the strange white bear. When he moved towards them they roared with terror and climbed to the very top of a tree, jostling one another in their haste.

The bravest of all were the fox cubs and the dingo puppies. These came close up to the bear cub's muzzle, but every time he tried to catch one of them they leaped aside agilely.

And so, though there were now many animals in the run, Fomka was again alone.

After a time we let in a tiger cub. Its name was Sirotka* because it had grown up without a mother.

The other cubs were afraid of Sirotka's powerful paw and sharp claws. But how was Fomka to know that? As· soon as we let Sirotka out, Fomka ran up to him. Sirotka spat at the newcomer, raising his paw threateningly. But the bear cub did not understand tiger language. He went nearer, and the next moment got such a box on the ear that he could hardly keep his feet.

* Little orphan.—*Tr.*

The treacherous blow infuriated Fomka. His head held low, he rushed at the offender with a loud roar.

When we hurried up to see what the noise was about, it was hard to see which was tiger and which was bear. They were grappling one another violently, roaring and rolling on the ground, tufts of white and orange fur flying about in all directions. At last we managed to separate the squabblers. We put them back in their cages, and only allowed them to come out again several days later.

This time we kept them under observation, but we need not have been afraid. Having taken each other's measure, they now treated each other with greater respect. Fomka let Sirotka severely alone, and Sirotka did not so much as raise a paw when he passed by.

And the other baby animals now treated Fomka quite differently. The brown bears tried to get him to wrestle with them and the wolf cubs and raccoons no longer ran away. But Fomka was not interested in them. He enjoyed chasing the fox cubs and the dingo puppies and wrestling with the bear cubs, but it was obvious that he was a great deal stronger than they were, and that his victories cost him little trouble. Fomka needed to measure his strength against an opponent equally strong. The only such opponent was Sirotka, who for his part took a great interest in Fomka himself.

They made friends gradually, while playing, and in a couple of weeks they were inseparable.

They spent the whole day together. It was interesting to watch their play. Sirotka was fond of hiding and suddenly jumping out on her playmate. Fomka would pass by and Sirotka would jump out, seize the cub by the scruff of the neck, worry him a bit, and then run away. But what Fomka liked was wrestling. He would seize the tiger cub in his paws, give him a powerful hug, and try to floor him. It is hard to escape from a bear's hug, but the little striped beast would not give in. He would press his front paws against Fomka's tummy, and try to push him away. There was always a crowd round the young animals' enclosure. Some of them came specially to watch the wrestling matches.

These matches usually ended in a draw. But one day Fomka got so tired of the tiger cub that he escaped from him into the water, and sat there cooling himself, while Sirotka walked round, unable to get at him. He walked up and down for a long time and then, suddenly losing his patience, gave a jump, missed his footing and fell into the water with a splash. This time he got a good punishing from Fomka, who was very much more at home in the water than the tiger. In less than a minute he got Sirotka down and dragged him along under water, almost drowning him. Wet and terrified, Sirotka tore himself from the bear's em-

brace and fled shamefacedly to his cage. After this, Sirotka was afraid of going too near the pool when Fomka was in it, and would not even drink when he was near.

But the incident did not in the least interfere with their friendship and they still spent most of the day playing together.

FOMKA BECOMES DANGEROUS

By the autumn Fomka had grown out of all knowledge. He still got on very well with the other animals in the enclosure, never hurt the weaker ones, and kept up his friendship with Sirotka, but he was not nearly so good with human beings as before. He had always been obedient, but now he would not even let Katya order him about.

Poor Katya! She had to use all sorts of tricks to make Fomka go into his cage when he did not want to.

The young animals were usually enticed into their cages with food. As soon as a bit of food was put inside they would run into them at once. But there was no luring Fomka. His stomach, always crammed with food, was as tight as a drum. He was given a snack for every little thing—for keeping away from the barrier, for not interfering with the cleaning of the cages, even for not biting. Fomka only had to look a little queer, and an attendant was sure to throw him something nice. And since he got paid with food for every little thing, by the end of the day he felt so full that he could not be tempted into his cage by the daintiest titbit.

Katya would spend a long time trying to persuade and distract him. Fomka was a very inquisitive bear. The moment he caught sight of anything unfamiliar he would hurry up to it to get a closer view.

Katya decided to take advantage of this. She would go into the cage and throw a kerchief, a jacket, or something of that sort on the floor. Then she would pretend to find it very interesting, touch it, pick it up. Sometimes she had to go on doing this for some time, it all depended on Fomka's mood. But other times he would go into the cage at once. Then Katya would deftly whisk away the bait from under his nose, and hurry out. But this was not always a success. Sometimes she did not get the thing away quickly enough, and then Fomka would deal with it in his own way.

The clever Fomka soon saw through this ruse, however, and it became harder every day to cope with the half-grown bear. After he once gave an attendant a bad bite it was decided to transfer him to the Animal Islet. We were sorry to part with Fomka, but it could not be helped, he had become too dangerous to be left in the enclosure.

On the Animal Islet there was a big empty run, with a large, deep pool in it. There was plenty of room to run about, to play and to bathe. And that was where Fomka went.

When Fomka found himself alone in a new place he was terrified. He hurled himself about the run, roaring piteously and looking for a way out. But there was no way out. Then Fomka curled up in a corner and would not come out of it even to be fed. After living in the young animals' enclosure, where he had had so many companions, he felt intensely lonely all by himself. He walked up and down and stopped playing altogether. But he was not lonely long. Soon another bear, Mashka, was brought to the Zoo and put with Fomka. She was much smaller than Fomka, but he did not hurt her. Snorting affectionately he sniffed at her and together they plunged into the water. All day they swam about and played, and when night came the cubs slept soundly, embracing one another with their paws.

Fomka was now quite happy. He enjoyed his life with his new friend—the polar bear cub, Mashka.

NAYA THE OTTER

FOSTER-BABY

NAYA WAS an otter. Her body was long and so flexible that there seemed to be no bones in it. Her head was flat like a snake's, and her tiny eyes were like beads. All this may sound as if Naya were an ugly little thing, but with her fluffy fur she was so sweet that one could not help wanting to stroke her.

I took Naya when she was quite a tiny otter. This sort of baby gives a lot of trouble. It has to be fed day and night, and if it is cold it has to have a hot-water bottle. I was on vacation just then and lived in the country, not far from Moscow. I took a great fancy to Naya and decided to adopt her and take her with me to the country.

The railway carriage was crowded. Finding an empty place with difficulty, I sat down. The otter lay in its basket, fast asleep, curled up in a ball. I set the basket down beside me and dozed. I was awakened by a piercing whistle. A woman sitting beside me recoiled with a loud cry. Everyone in the carriage turned to look at me. I only understood what had happened when there was a second whistle. The cause of the excitement turned out to be little Naya. Tired of sitting in the cramped basket she had jumped out, and was whistling for her mother.

Putting her back in the basket, I went into the next carriage, and the rest of the journey passed without mishap.

My little boy, Tolya, was gladder than anyone else in the family to see Naya. He had read in a book that otters swim and catch fish marvellously, and now he had a real baby otter of his own. He assured us that when Naya grew up she would catch fish for him.

Tolya undertook to look after Naya. He made a warm comfortable nest for her in the corner next to his bed, gave her some milk, and put her to bed. Naya fell asleep almost instantly, lying on her side with one paw under her head, just like a human being. She always slept like this, or flat on her back with her paws folded over her stomach. Tolya would cover her with a small blanket, and she looked very quaint.

Naya soon got used to us, and knew each of us by our voices and footsteps. The moment anyone came to the door she would go running up, expressing her joy with bird-like chirpings. Naya was an affectionate, happy little creature. She spent almost all her time playing—turning somersaults and trying to catch her own tail. Her favourite plaything was Tolya's plush dog. She would throw herself upon it as if it were her prey, worry at its big, soft ears, run back, her long tail held high, and rush at it again. Or else, lying on her back, she would embrace the dog with her front paws and pretend to wrestle with it. Between her paws the dog almost seemed to come alive, jumping, attacking, and retreating. When she got tired, Naya fell asleep beside her toy. If it was taken away from her she would miss it, and go all over the room looking for it, whimpering softly.

IN HER NATIVE ELEMENT

When Naya grew bigger we began giving her fish as well as milk. At first we boned it and cut it up fine, a little later we gave it to her whole, and at last alive. Children, who took a great interest in the baby otter, brought minnows for her. They would wait patiently in front of our house for someone to come out and take Naya for a walk.

Naya liked playing with them and never bit them. Soon she had many friends among them. I would come home and find the door hung all over with bunches of minnows and little notes: "For Naya from Kolya." "Let Naya eat this and grow big! Styopa Ivanov." "V. Fedosyev brought these minnows." There was a note with every bunch. Live minnows were supplied, too. They came in glass jars full of water and were left on the doorstep. I would constantly come out of the house and step right into a jar, sending minnows flying in one direction, and the jar in another, while the water trickled down the steps.

Naya was very fond of live fish. We would pour some water into a basin and empty some minnows into it. When Naya caught sight of the fish in the basin there was no holding her. Wriggling out of our arms like an eel, she would dive into the basin, splashing the water in all directions. We could not see which was fish and which was

123

Katya decided to take advantage of this. She would go into the cage and throw a kerchief, a jacket, or something of that sort on the floor. Then she would pretend to find it very interesting, touch it, pick it up. Sometimes she had to go on doing this for some time, it all depended on Fomka's mood. But other times he would go into the cage at once. Then Katya would deftly whisk away the bait from under his nose, and hurry out. But this was not always a success. Sometimes she did not get the thing away quickly enough, and then Fomka would deal with it in his own way.

The clever Fomka soon saw through this ruse, however, and it became harder every day to cope with the half-grown bear. After he once gave an attendant a bad bite it was decided to transfer him to the Animal Islet. We were sorry to part with Fomka, but it could not be helped, he had become too dangerous to be left in the enclosure.

On the Animal Islet there was a big empty run, with a large, deep pool in it. There was plenty of room to run about, to play and to bathe. And that was where Fomka went.

But Naya's hearing was excellent. If Tolya did not move, she would whistle once or twice and wait, and getting no answer would go to her own place to sleep. If, however, Tolya moved the least little bit, Naya would rush to him and again beg to be taken into his bed.

She hated being left alone. When we went for walks she would make such a noise that we had to take her with us.

Naya loved going for walks, running after us like a dog, keeping up with us all the time. We went everywhere with her, but we were afraid to go near the river, in case Naya, catching sight of the water, dived in and never came back.

One day we went with her to the woods. Naya soon got tired of running after us on her short legs and begged to be put into her basket, where she fell asleep. We found a lot of mushrooms on the way, and did not know where to put them. Of course we ended by putting them in the basket, till Naya was quite covered up.

It was a hot, sunny day. We decided to go and bathe, quite forgetting that there was an otter asleep in the basket, under the mushrooms. We went to the river, and started undressing. Suddenly the basket began to move, mushrooms were scattered over the ground, and before I had time to realize what had happened, Naya was on the bank of the river.

"Naya! Naya! Naya!" cried Tolya and I.

But Naya did not so much as turn her head. She was at the water's edge in a flash, and plunged headlong into the river. For some time we could see her, then she dived and disappeared. We ran along the bank shouting and calling to her. Naya was nowhere to be seen.

Tolya was more upset than any of us. He could not bear to go home without Naya, and kept running along the bank, looking for her.

The day was drawing to a close. It was obviously no use waiting any longer, and we were just going to turn back when Naya's shrill whistle was heard up the river some distance away.

"Naya, Naya, Naya!" we shouted joyously, all together.

The whistling came nearer and nearer. And suddenly Naya appeared from behind a bend in the river, cleaving the water with strong strokes. She swam so quickly that she seemed to be skimming over the surface of the water. Every now and then she gave a sort of leap, turning her head from side to side and whistling shrilly.

Throwing off his clothes as he ran, Tolya rushed straight into the water to meet her. Naya swam up to him as soon as she caught sight of him. She could not contain her delight, climbing on to Tolya's shoulders, diving under him, and rubbing against his face with loving grunts. Then they both clambered on to the shore, and Naya proceeded to dry herself on the clothes lying on the grass. She rolled herself on Tolya's new suit, leaving wet, dirty streaks on it, but no one scolded her. Ever since that day we always took Naya to bathe with us, and nobody was afraid any more that she would swim away.

IN THE ZOO

But the warm summer days were coming to an end. Autumn came and we went back to Moscow, taking Naya with us. After the freedom of the countryside the otter was unhappy in a cramped town flat. She fretted, kept begging to be let out into the passage, and then back again into the room, missing the freedom she had become accustomed to. Now she had to bathe in a trough. After her bath Naya would climb on to a bed or an armchair to dry herself. It became impossible to keep her in the house any longer. Besides, Tolya had started going to school and there was nobody to look after her.

So Naya had to be taken to the Zoo. I took her myself, without Tolya. Naya was put in a spacious cage with a large, deep pool. She seemed to be quite happy in her new home, and plunged into the water immediately, diving, turning somersaults, swimming. Then I went quietly out of the cage, closing the door behind me. But quietly as I moved Naya heard me and dashed out of the water. At first she tried to squeeze through the bars, and to gnaw at them. Then she pressed her whole body against the cold metal bars and began whining in a thin shrill voice.

For some time neither Tolya nor I went to the Zoo. Tolya felt the parting with Naya keenly, and nothing but the thought that she would be happier at the Zoo than at home could comfort him. He grieved for her so deeply that even when I went to the Zoo two months later, he would not go with me.

"I'm sure to cry. I'd better not go."

So I had to go alone.

Once inside the Zoo I hastened to Naya's cage and stood so that she should not see me. Just then the attendant went into her cage. Naya ran up to him, rose on her hind legs and begged for food. The attendant took a big fish out of his bucket and threw it into the water. Naya caught it at once, took it out of the water and started eating. Then, so softly that I could hardly hear my own voice, I called her.

Naya started, raised her head a little and seemed to be all ears. I kept silent. Naya gave a harsh cry, and then paused, as if waiting for an answer. Her small eyes searched restlessly for me among the crowd. I could hold out no longer and ran up to the cage, and Naya ran to meet me, pushing her paws between the bars and trying to catch hold of my hands. After this I went to see her every day.

While the attendant opened the door for me, Naya, chirping impatiently, ran up and down in front of it. She would get into my lap, showing her affection in all sorts of ways, and only then begin to play. It was winter, and Naya's games were quite different from her summer games. Her pool was covered with a thick layer of ice, but this did not prevent her from bathing.

Just as before she would jump into the water as if inviting me to follow her, diving in by one hole and coming out by another. Or she would get to the top of a little mound and slide down on her belly. She made a real slide from a snowy mound right on the edge of the pool. Leaping out of the water she would clamber all wet, without shaking herself, on to the snow. Streams of water trickled down from her body, freezing immediately, and she went backwards and forwards from the water to the snow, till she had made it into a slide. Down this slide Naya tobogganed. Lying on her belly or on her back, she slid down it into the water. It made one cold only to look at her. There was I with my nose buried in my coat collar, and Naya, not minding the frost a bit, bathing as if it were summer. Her gleaming fur was so smooth and dense that it did not hold the water. Naya only had to jump out and shake herself, and she was dry again.

Naya was very careful not to let her holes get covered. If they began to freeze she broke the crust with her head, or nibbled at the edges. As well as the big holes she had air holes in the ice, tiny apertures through which she could breathe under the ice. At first I knew nothing about these, but one day Naya stayed a long time under water. I was worried, afraid something might have happened. I began looking for her. Suddenly I saw that the snow had melted a little in one place and that steam was rising from it. I went nearer and heard heavy breathing under the ice—it was Naya hiding from me, her nose pressed against the vent. Later I found several of these little openings.

They were very small, but they did not close up even in the keenest frost, for Naya took a great deal of trouble at such times to prevent her icy domain from freezing over.

Naya made herself a hole in the snow to sleep in and a tunnel from it leading straight to the water. She was very fond of digging in the snow.

On my free days I used to take her out for a walk. We walked along the paths around the big pond in the Zoo. The pond is railed off, but Naya made no attempt to get into it anyhow. What she liked best of all was to burrow into snow-drifts, and sometimes I would be walking along the path, she keeping up with me under the snow. But I only had to turn into another path for Naya to push her way out of the snow and run along by my side.

I used to wonder how she could hear that I had turned away, beneath the deep snow.

Naya loved making snowballs, especially when there was soft, new-fallen snow. Finding a small lump of snow, she would start rolling it in front of her with the tip of her nose, until it had grown into a big ball. Sometimes it would become so big that Naya could not make it budge. Then she would throw herself on it, gnawing at it, and breaking it up with her paws.

Naya enjoyed the walks, but they soon had to be given up. One day when we were walking as usual near the pond, Naya crawled under the railings and ran to a hole in the ice. I was terribly alarmed. There were ducks, swans, geese, and many other waterfowl swimming about the hole. They might be frightened away by Naya and take to flight, or she might bite them. When the birds saw the otter there was a terrific hullabaloo. Ducks, geese and red-breasted barnacles flew up in all directions with loud cries and the flapping of wings. Naya was on the point of turning back when she was attacked by the swans. One of them struck her so violently with its wings that she rolled head over heels. Then the other swans attacked her, beating her, and flinging her backwards and forwards like a football.

I rushed to her aid, but could do nothing. The infuriated birds would very likely have beaten Naya to death if one of the blows had not sent her rolling into the water.

She tried several times to get to me, but whenever her head appeared above the water the swans drove her back.

I rescued her with great difficulty, after driving the swans off, but after this the walks had to be given up. Naya missed them badly. When I passed her cage she would run beside me inside the railings, with plaintive cries. I had to go round by another way, so as not to upset her.

FLIGHT

Winter passed and spring came, bringing with it warm sunny days. Naya had become a full-grown handsome beast, and when an otter was needed for a film, she was chosen. A picture of animal life had to be made, showing among other things how otters swim and catch fish under water. Naya was the obvious choice. She was not afraid of human beings, knew her name well, and, most important of all, was not alarmed by the camera's rat-tat-tat. Wild animals are often so terrified by this unfamiliar sound that they run away and hide, and it is hard to film them, but Naya paid not the slightest heed to it.

Preparations for the picture began. A special aquarium was made to photograph the otter under water. It was so huge that twelve men could hardly get it off the lorry and set it up. River sand, shells and water-plants were put on the bottom of the aquarium. Then three jupiter-lights and two cameras were placed so as to photograph from two sides at once. When I peeped into the view-finder I got the impression of a section of a real river, and I would never have believed it was only an aquarium.

Everything was in readiness. The attendant brought Naya in a small cage and let her into the water. I had often seen the otter swim, but never before under water. I had no idea her movements could be so soft and plastic. Stretching to her full length she pressed her front paws against her body and extended her hind legs in a straight line with her tail. Long, snake-like, she slipped like a shadow between the water-plants. Her nostrils, usually so restless, were tightly compressed to keep out the water, and her small, bead-like eyes gleamed. A fish was thrown into the aquarium. Naya gave no sign of having seen it. Her movements were as plastic as ever and she even seemed to be slowing down. But when she got on a level with the fish she made an abrupt pouncing movement and snapped it up. A big, powerful fish, it lashed with its tail, trying to break away, but the sharp, crooked teeth of the otter held their prey securely.

After the underwater pictures had been taken, the otter had to be photographed going into the water. For this purpose a special cage was made on the Zoo's New Territory. It included an artificial river, and water-plants like those among which otters live when at liberty. The banks of the little river were planted with sedge and bushes, and an old hollow oak-tree with exposed roots, looking as though the tree had been torn up by a storm, was laid on the ground. It was a picturesque wild nook. The railings were invisible, being camouflaged with foliage. In a word, everything was done to make this corner of the Zoo look like a bit of the real countryside.

The first thing Naya did in the new place was to explore her cage. She examined every blade of grass, every bush and tree, got into the hollow of the oak, and tried in vain to burrow underneath the railings.

Then she investigated the net and there was not a single opening in its mesh that she did not try to squeeze herself through. And when they came to film the otter the next morning, the cage was empty.

Naya was sought for everywhere, but nobody could find her.

It grew dark and the search had to be put off till the next day.

That night there was terrific commotion among the waterfowl on the pond. A night watchman came running up to see what was wrong. He caught sight of the long narrow shadow of an otter slipping into the water, and next morning the remains of a half-gnawed duck and an otter's tracks showed that the night had not been wasted for her.

There were red-breasted barnacle geese in the New Territory. These are extremely rare and valuable birds and, since Naya could have killed off the whole flock, it was then decided to catch her dead or alive.

Naya was at large five days. In the day-time she hid among the reeds of the pond, and at night she went hunting. The night watchmen tried again and again to catch her but she slipped through their fingers with the utmost agility. It was a night watchman who told me that Naya had run away, as I was passing through the New Territory on my way home.

"Naya, Naya, Naya!" I called, as I went by the pond, just as I used to call her on our walks.

And Naya, who had for five days defied all attempts to catch her, responded to my cry with her familiar whistle. Whistling and cleaving the water, terrifying all the birds in her way, she swam up to me. And she followed me obediently into the cage, as if we were back in the old times, when she was a baby otter and we went for walks together.

Several years passed. The war began. The animals had to be evacuated.

132

A barge loaded with animals floated down the Volga, when three German aeroplanes swooped down on it one after another.

One of the high-explosive bombs fell wide of the barge, but another hit the bow, where the cages of the animals were. Among them was Naya. Many animals were killed immediately, many were thrown into the water, or thrashed in terror all over the deck.

Who can tell what became of Naya? Whether she was killed amongst the fragments of the barge, or whether she went back to live in her native element, I do not know. But I often think of the little otter that used to live in our home.

KUTSI*

KUTSI WAS a lean fox with very long legs.
He had high pointed ears and eyes a little aslant, and there always seemed to be a smile on his face. He did not have a bushy tail, like a fox. Instead of the long brush which is the fox's glory, he had a little stump. And this gave him a particularly cheeky look.

He was brought to the Zoo by a hunter.

There were a great many foxes in the cage where Kutsi was put, but this did not seem to bother him, though it usually upsets newcomers. He seemed to feel quite at home in the new place and when one of the vixens snapped at him, Kutsi turned sharply, grabbed the aggres-

* Stumpy.—*Tr.*

sor by the scruff of the neck and gave her such a shaking that after this neither she nor any of the other foxes dared to go near him again. As for Lyona, who looked after the foxes, Kutsi treated him from the first as if he had known him all his life.

When Lyona came into the cage Kutsi would scamper up to him, wag his stump of a tail and look lovingly into his face, as if expecting to be petted. And it must be admitted that Lyona took much more notice of him than he did of the other foxes, and often gave him the best pieces of meat. So it will be seen that Kutsi was well able to adapt himself to the ups and downs of life. Kutsi had yet another peculiarity which impressed us all very much—he was a great lover of freedom, and could escape from any cage.

Kutsi ran away the first time about a fortnight after he was brought to the Zoo. When the attendant came to clean the cage, there was no Kutsi in it. For a long time Lyona could not understand where he had got to. There was no hole in the cage, and all the other foxes were there. Then the attendant guessed what had happened—inside the cage, next to the bars, there grew a tree, the top of which stuck out of a hole made for it in the roof of the cage. And through this hole Kutsi must have escaped. He had managed it with wonderful cunning—pressing his back against the trunk of the tree (there were even some tufts of fur left on the bark), he had clambered up the wire netting, as if it were a ladder. Lyona could only shake his head in astonishment. He had never come across such a cunning fox before.

"Who would have thought a little beast like that could be so artful?" he exclaimed.

Kutsi was brought back in a day or two. A man brought him in a basket tied up in a shawl. And after him trailed a little crowd of children. Many of them had bites on their hands, and so they were very much surprised when Lyona picked up Kutsi fearlessly and Kutsi did not touch him. He did not even bite Lyona when the old man tweaked his ear.

Kutsi was put back in the cage. The opening through which he had escaped was closed, but this did not prevent him from running away again.

This time he simply went through the door. Hardly had Lyona opened it, one day, when Kutsi bounded with lightning speed between his legs and disappeared, with a twitch of his stumpy tail.

A regular expedition was sent to look for the truant. But they failed to catch Kutsi. Not for nothing had he explored the Zoo so thoroughly. Kutsi was given up for lost, and his name struck off the feeding register. A few more days went by. Then ducks began to disappear regularly from the two ponds in the Zoo. It was impossible to discover the offender, for the snow was trampled all over and no tracks could be seen on it.

The nocturnal thief was exposed quite by chance.

One morning when Lyona came to the cage, he saw that there was something wrong with his foxes. They were all crowded against the front of the cage, squabbling, thrusting their paws through the bars, trying to get something from under the snow. Lonya came nearer, and there was a dead duck sticking out of the snow. "Could it be the duck that was missing from the pond last night?" he said to himself. He picked it up and took it to the manager. The manager examined it and found it was the very duck which had disappeared the night before. It was established that it had been killed by a fox. And now everything seemed to point to Kutsi. Very soon the suspicions were confirmed. There was a fall of snow and the imprints of fox-pads could be clearly seen on the snow beside the pond. Again the hunt for Kutsi was up. But it proved no easy matter to find the runaway. Nobody knew where he had gone. A hound was set on his tracks,

136

traps were laid and a watch kept night after night, but Kutsi was not to be caught. And every night a dead bird was found on the bank of the ponds.

Kutsi came back of his own accord in the simplest possible manner. One morning, when the attendant came to clean the cage, there was

Kutsi, waiting outside with the most affectionate welcome, as if nothing whatever had happened.

Apparently he had got tired of leading a vagrant life and made up his mind to go home. While Lyona was unlocking the door of the cage Kutsi pranced round him with obvious impatience. Such a display of the fox's repentance touched Lyona deeply, and Kutsi was there and then forgiven all his sins, and all the ducks he had killed.

The first few days after his return Kutsi was a model of propriety. He did not quarrel and showed not the slightest desire to run away. But this was only a breathing space. The next time he escaped in quite a new way. He dug under the wire netting and left the cage, taking all the other foxes with him. The rest were quickly captured, but it was not so easy to catch Kutsi. He was found several days later on the New Territory, in the bears' enclosure.

He must have got there by accident. Probably he had not noticed the wide, deep moat separating the bears from visitors, and fallen into it. When we got there we found all the three bears chasing Kutsi. And Kutsi seemed to be mocking them. The bears' enclosure is very spacious and Kutsi had no trouble in dodging the clumsy bears. He walked slowly away from them, as if teasing them, sometimes sitting down and waiting for the bears to come quite near, when he dived under their bellies and got away.

Once the bears all but caught him. Two of them ran up to him from opposite sides. One had already raised its paw to strike him, and it seemed as if Kutsi's last hour had come, but the cunning fox ducked under the bear's paw and slipped out between its hind legs. In their astonishment the bears banged their heads against each other and started fighting. They knocked each other about and then, thoroughly bewildered, began a long search for the culprit. We came and went several times, but the bears never stopped chasing Kutsi. They were so exhausted that their panting could be heard from the other side of the moat. And the fox seemed to be making fun of them all the time—jumping over their shaggy backs, diving under their bellies, and getting away every time.

At last the bears grew weary of the fruitless chase and gave it up.

It was a warm, sunny day. The poor Mishkas* slid into the pool, quite worn out. They splashed about for a time in the cool water. They rolled over first on one side, then on the other, floated on their backs and seemed to have forgotten all about the fox, when the attendant arrived with their food. Then all three bears got out of the water at once. Each took up his usual place, received his portion of meat, and fell to. They were munching away peacefully when suddenly Kutsi appeared. He evidently did not intend to go without his dinner and walked resolutely up to the bears.

They took no notice of the impudent fox, but Kutsi ran round and round them, and right under their noses, trying to snatch some meat— if only a very little bit. But bears are greedy animals. They had not the least desire to share their meal with the uninvited guest. Roaring angrily they covered the meat with their paws, turned their backs to Kutsi, and tried to shove him away. Seeing that no meat was to be got by fair means, the "guest" chose a moment and snapped at the heel of one of the "hosts." Then there was a regular hullabaloo! The infuriated bear, not seeing who had bitten him, fell violently on his neighbour, and in a moment the food was scattered, the bears were fighting, and Kutsi settled himself comfortably on a rock to enjoy a huge bit of meat. The attendants had trouble in separating the bears, and only managed to do so by throwing fire-crackers at them. Animals are very

* *Mishka*, Bruin.—*Tr.*

much afraid of fire-crackers, and when they heard the explosions the bears immediately ran into their cages. There they were locked up. Then the attendants began chasing Kutsi with a net. But they did not succeed. Not for nothing had three bears been unable to catch him in the course of a whole day. Every time an attempt was made to slip the net over him, the fox wriggled away or ran up the almost sheer slope at the back of the enclosure and jumped back over the heads of his pursuers.

Lyona had to be sent for. Kutsi recognized him at once, ran up to him, and quietly allowed himself to be picked up.

"Kutsi, Kutsi, our cage is too cramped for you! Oh, how you love your freedom!" sighed Lyona.

He went to the manager and asked permission to transfer the restless fox to another cage. He was sorry to part with the clever fox, but it could not be helped—he really gave too much trouble with his escapades.

The cage into which Kutsi was transferred was strong and spacious.

It stood in the young animals' enclosure, which was itself railed off with high bars surmounted by a ledge. So Kutsi was kept in a cage within a cage.

This enclosure was specially made for the animals to roam about freely in, but we were afraid to let Kutsi into it.

The lively, playful fox pined in solitude. When the other animals were let out into the enclosure he begged to be allowed to join them, whined, and even lost his appetite. Everybody pitied Kutsi.

"Well, why not let him out, after all?" said Tanya, a new attendant.

We argued with her, telling her that she was not up to Kutsi's tricks, but Tanya stuck to her guns.

At last, after long arguments, it was decided to let Kutsi out. The door was opened. Kutsi strolled quietly out of the cage, as if it were the most every day occurrence, and went slowly up to the bars. It was easy to guess what the fox's intentions were. They could be read in his confident gait and in the look of his eyes. Kutsi ran up to a corner of the enclosure, and before anyone realized what he was up to, jumped straight from the ground on to the ledge.

There was quite a crowd outside the enclosure. When they saw a fox on the ledge they began shouting, waving their hands, trying to frighten Kutsi away. But this did not upset him in the least. Without paying the slightest attention to anyone he jumped right into the crowd, slipped deftly between the legs of the onlookers and ran off along the path.

Everyone rushed after him, Tanya in the lead. Several times she almost caught Kutsi up. This was not, of course, because Kutsi was a poor runner. When Tanya fell behind, the fox, as if on purpose, slowed down.

He got as far as the railing round the Zoo. And then ... then Kutsi turned once more, waved his stump of a tail and squeezed through the railings. Since then nobody has ever seen him. This was the last escape of the stump-tailed fox with a passion for freedom.

AN ORDINARY PUSSY

IT IS WELL KNOWN that cats and rats are sworn foes. That used to be my opinion, too. But the time came when I had to admit that this is not always true.

Friendship between a cat and baby rats had to be screened for a scientific film. Children brought cats of all sorts to us several days running, but none of them were any good. Some were too light-coloured, some too dark. At last, after a lot of trouble, the right one was found—an ordinary tabby with bright green eyes. The producer took to her at once—it was just the cat he required. But his joy was short-lived. The cat was brought to us by a little boy, but her mistress would not hear of parting with her pet. Besides, the cat had kittens.

The producer was in despair. He begged the owner of Pussy to let him have her, offering a good price and promising to give the cat back directly after the filming.

"Your cat is just the right colouring," he pleaded. "We'll only screen her friendship with rats and give her back at once."

"With rats!" exclaimed the owner. "Why, I don't want to give her up, chiefly because she's such a splendid ratter. She has caught all the rats, not only in my house, but in the neighbour's too, and you want her to make friends with them. Why, she'll gobble them all up at once!"

To tell the truth, this description of the future "star" rather dismayed me. I had often enough given cats and dogs various baby animals to nurse, but had never had to give baby rats to a cat famous as a ratter. I, too, began to persuade the producer not to take her, but he insisted on having his own way.

And this is how a cat who was very good at catching rats came to the Zoo with her whole family.

Someone gave her the name of Tsutsikarikha. Why this name had been chosen, nobody knew, but it stuck to the cat.

At the Zoo the cat family was put into a special cage.

At first Tsutsikarikha was very uneasy in her new home. She ran about the cage, mewing and looking for a way out. Then she grew quieter, and lay down with her kittens. In a few days' time we brought in the baby rats for whom Tsutsikarikha was to act as a mother. They were tiny creatures, covered with an almost invisible film of fur, and their eyes were not yet open.

They wriggled in my hands in a little bunch, and I stood in front of Tsutsikarikha's cage, wondering how she would receive them. When I went into the cage, the cat immediately got their scent. She sprang up and began walking round and round me, every now and then

143

standing on her hind legs and trying to get at my hands. Seeing how the rats excited her, I did not dare to leave them with her.

Another way had to be found.

Tsutsikarikha was put in a box and taken to another room, and the rats were placed with the kittens. I did this on purpose. "She will miss her kittens," I thought, "and then she won't mind some other animals being amongst them. And the rats will smell of the kittens."

My reasoning turned out to be correct. A few hours later Tsutsikarikha began mewing at the top of her voice, and by the evening there was a concert that had to be heard to be believed. She mewed and scratched at the walls, the kittens squealed, and amongst them groped the tiny rats, blindly seeking their mother's teats.

When I let Tsutsikarikha out of her captivity she rushed like mad to her kittens, and immediately lay down, without paying the slightest attention to the rats. Stretching blissfully, she shut her eyes and purred. This was the most suitable moment to put the rats to her teats. Gently, so as not to alarm her, I took one kitten to the next room, and then, just as cautiously, put a baby rat to the teat. The cat went on purring without noticing the change. In this way I put the rest of the rats to her teats—the kittens were placed under the care of the attendant, Katya.

And so a cat began peacefully living with baby rats. The rats were not a bit like kittens, but the "famous ratter" looked after them like a mother. She kept them warm, washed their fur, and protected them when any danger threatened.

One day a tomcat strolled into the room in which Tsutsikarikha and the baby rats were being photographed.

It was an enormous black cat, very imposing, with fierce whiskers and a scar on his forehead. But Tsutsikarikha was not a bit afraid of him. She rushed boldly to the defence of her unusual family and

before the tom knew where he was, a hail of blows landed on him. At first he tried to defend himself, but soon saw how useless this was, and retreated in disgrace. He fled across the room, his tail streaming behind him, pursued by the infuriated mamma, and after them, vainly trying to catch the "star," ran the producer, the cameraman, and all the rest.

But nobody could catch the cat, and only when she had driven the enemy under a heap of scenery in a corner, did Tsutsikarikha calm down and come back. She sniffed at the rats and, having made sure that they were all safe and sound, lay down beside them. She purred so lovingly and licked her foster-children so solicitously that no one could have recognized in her the fury of a few minutes before.

When the baby rats grew up they were transferred with the cat into another cage, where they could be seen by visitors.

Day after day people crowded in front of the extraordinary family. Everyone wanted to look at the "miracle." All sorts of remarks were overheard. Some suggested that there must be something wrong with the cat, that its teeth had probably been pulled out.... But Pussy opened her mouth in a great yawn, showing her sharp fangs, and cuddled up with the rats again.

Tsutsikarikha's mistress came, but did not take her back. She glanced at her former pet and shrugged her shoulders.

"You've spoilt my cat. What a fine ratter she was!"

And the "fine ratter" lay in the sun, with baby rats climbing fearlessly over her. We tried to console the distressed owner by telling her that it was only "her own" rats the cat would not hurt, and that she would still catch other rats, but when we looked on this tranquil picture, we did not believe our own words.

One day, however, we realized that we need not have had any doubts. We let Tsutsikarikha out of her cage for a walk. At first she stayed close to the cage, and then suddenly vanished. We were alarmed, thinking she had gone for good. But a little time after Tsutsikarikha returned, a big dead rat in her teeth. She walked with dignified, unhurried steps up to the cage, and when she was let in, spent a long time thrusting her prey towards the baby rats.

It was very interesting to see the cat playing with her foster-children. Their tails erect, jumping on all four legs, as if on springs, the rats would advance upon Tsutsikarikha, who caught them, tossed them about like balls, rolled them over on the ground, and sometimes seized one between her teeth as if she meant to gobble it up. This always caused a stir among the spectators, but the cat, purring again, would lick the ruffled fur of the baby rat.

146

After they had lived together almost the whole summer, an attendant forgot to shut the door of the cage one day, and the rats escaped.

Oh, what a to-do there was! The cat mewed, dashing about the cage looking for the rats, who had got under the floor, and were afraid to come out. We tried to reach them, but it was quite impossible. Then it was decided to let Pussy out, to see if she could catch her rats herself. As soon as the door was opened, she leaped out and made straight for the corner. There she crouched, waiting, nothing but the tip of her tail stirring. And I, too, waited breathlessly. "What if I am unable to get the rats away from her alive?" I thought. There we sat, each on the watch—the cat watching the rats, I watching the cat. All of a sudden Pussy pounced. I was after her immediately. But it's not so easy to catch a cat! She slipped through my hands straight into the cage, her eyes blazing, a baby rat between her teeth. "It's all up with the poor thing!" I said to myself. "She'll eat it." But what I saw astonished me. Tsutsikarikha, after looking for a convenient place, lay down and began licking the rat! And as she licked it she kept looking round as if afraid someone would take it away. Then she calmed down and went to catch another. Again she crouched and watched, but I was no longer afraid, I knew she would not hurt her rats.

By the evening the cat had caught them all but one, which—little coward!—was afraid to come out of its hole, though in the night, when everyone had gone away, it gnawed at the bars, trying vainly to get back to its home.

Now the cat had only three babies instead of four.

They lived together a long, long time. On cold winter nights the cat kept the baby rats warm with the heat of her body, and shared her food with them. I never saw a more loving family. And now, when I am told that cats and rats are sworn foes, I reply that even natural enemies can become friends.

10*

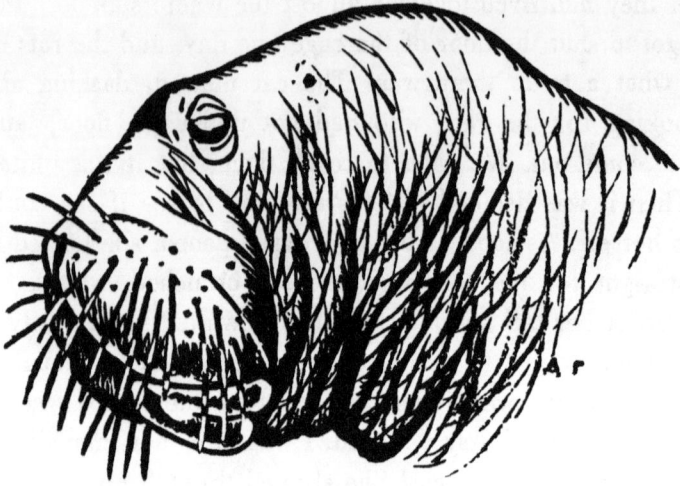

NURKA

NURKA WAS a queer creature. She was fat and snub-nosed, and, like all walruses, she had a bristly moustache sticking out all round. This, and her round moist eyes gave her a very amusing expression— stupid but most dignified. But she only seemed stupid. In reality Nurka was very intelligent.

She had come to the Moscow Zoo from the Island of Wrangel, making the long, hard journey by steamer and by train in a cramped box, without a chance to get to the water. She arrived in an emaciated condition with great open sores on her back and sides.

She was put into my charge and I washed her sores, cleaned out her cage, and gave her her food. I fed her on fish, which first had to be boned and cut into tiny pieces, for Nurka was still just a baby, if she *was* a walrus! She didn't even know how to eat. She took the food from my hand bit by bit, and sucked it in, making a noise like a cork popping out of a bottle. She ate from nine to eleven pounds of fish a day, sometimes even more. And as well as this she got a glass of cod-liver oil a day.

Nurka soon got fond of me, probably because I looked after her and fed her. She recognized me from a distance, greeting me with short, hollow yaps rather like the barking of a dog, and hurrying towards me, wobbling clumsily from side to side on her flippers.

The baby walrus was very intelligent. Not many dogs have better brains than Nurka.

For instance: Nurka hated me to go and leave her all by herself. The moment I moved towards the door she would bar the way, uttering angry cries. She seemed to think I ought to live with her. Sometimes I got quite cross—I was in such a hurry, there was so much to do, and she wouldn't let me open the door. I had to find ruses for getting away.

Nurka could eat by herself now, so I took some food and put it in a corner at the very back of the cage, and while she was eating ran away as fast as I could. But this did not work long, for Nurka soon saw through it. In a very few days she dived into her pool as soon as I turned to go, and of course she could swim across it quicker than I could walk round it. She would then flump her whole body against the door to prevent me from opening it. And just you try moving away a fat creature like her, weighing twenty-five stone! Nurka usually kept me a prisoner till she had played with me to her heart's content. And of course her notion of a game was not mine. She tried to get me to go into the pool with her, and when I wouldn't she would start shoving me with her nose. She didn't like getting into the water all alone. The pool was small and inconvenient, and she got bored in it all by herself.

Nurka spent most of the day sleeping on the bank of the pool. I decided to take her for walks so as to give her some exercise.

But this was not so easy as it sounds. Nurka simply refused to get out of her cage.

I opened the door, went out, and called her. She gave impatient cries and thrust her nose out, but could not make up her mind to cross the threshold.

I had to get her used to the idea gradually. I tempted her with fish, giving her a bit for every step she took. And so, step by step, we went farther and farther away. We did not stay out long. Nurka grazed her flippers on the gravel, and anyhow she could not walk long. Still, she got fond of going for walks.

We went out in the evenings, when the last visitors had left and the attendants' whistles had given notice of the closing of the Zoo. These whistles were the signal for Nurka to start looking for me to appear on one of the paths. When I got to her cage she would fling herself on the door to help me open it, and when I took the padlock off, she shoved at the door with her nose. She even learned to lift the latch. When I wanted to clean the cage I would turn Nurka out to get her out of the way, and fasten the latch from the inside. At first she used to utter loud cries and try to get in again, but she soon found a way to outwit me. She pushed up the latch with a blow of her snout and opened the door. She could aim very powerful blows with her snout.

Once, I remember, Nurka was ill and the doctor came to see her. She was very mistrustful of him, craning her neck in his direction, opening her mouth wide, and roaring threateningly. I warned the doctor not to touch her, but he took no notice of what I said and went

up to her with outstretched hand. Before he could touch her Nurka shoved him aside with a violent blow of her head.

Even I had not expected such a display of strength from her. Ever since then Nurka would not let the doctor come near her.

The pool froze over in the winter and Nurka was transferred to an indoor cage. An attendant now looked after her, instead of me.

He at once took to fat, clumsy Nurka. He was always giving her an extra bit of fish and petting her, and did not like it at all that Nurka knew me better than she did him.

"Don't come so often," he asked me. "Let her forget you."

I stopped visiting Nurka, so as not to offend the old attendant and give Nurka time to get used to him.

A month passed. I missed my quaint friend, and I couldn't help wondering if she would know me again. One day, passing the seal house, I decided to go in.

Nurka was lying under the water. She was quite invisible, but for the tip of her nose which every now and then came to the surface.

I called Nurka very softly, but she recognized my voice at once, even under the water. She could be very agile when she chose! In less than a minute Nurka was on dry ground, hoisting herself on to her hind flippers, and before I could step back, two heavy front flippers were weighing my shoulders down.

Streams of water ran down my coat, a wet whiskered face was thrust affectionately into mine and it was all I could do to keep on my feet.

It's no joke when a mountain of flesh like that leans against you. She almost suffocated me in her joy. I had the greatest difficulty in getting away.

When I went away Nurka shuffled up to the bars of the cage, looking after me and moaning piteously long after I had gone. They told me that there were real tears running down her face, and she would not eat that day.

One night Nurka pressed her heavy body against the wire netting till she got it loose, and went out into the corridor. Opening one door after another, she climbed the steep stairs to the attic and got out on to the roof through a trapdoor. Then her loud cries were heard in the stillness of the night. A watchman caught sight of her. Several men carried Nurka down, carefully slung on towels, and put her back where she belonged.

She never broke the netting down again or went out, and nobody could understand why she did so that night.

CHUZHOI

ONE COLD DAY in February the collie Perry gave birth to a litter of puppies. Nobody had known that she was going to have them. It was a cold, frosty day and all the puppies died. The poor dog, left all alone, mourned for a long time, whining and refusing food. Her teats swelled painfully, so I decided to give her a dingo puppy. The dingo is a wild Australian dog. The dingo mother had six little ones. All but one of them were sturdy little creatures. And this one was very small and puny. The mother was not so good to it as she was to the others, not washing it so often or looking after it properly, and when the poor little thing crawled up to her she often pushed it away with her nose.

It grew up sickly and feeble, the last to open its eyes, the last to begin walking. And so I decided to give it to Perry. But this could not be done without some preparations.

The dog had to be moved to a warm building. There was an empty room in the elephant house. I partitioned off a corner, laid some straw on the ground, and let Perry in. She did not lie down at once, but walked about the room, sniffing at all the corners, before settling down quietly in the place prepared for her. Then I brought the dingo pup to her.

The dog did not give the strange puppy a very kind welcome. It was much bigger than her lost babies, and its colour was quite different. The dingo pup kept running after her to be petted, but Perry growled, snapped and went away from it. I was afraid to leave them together in the night. We had to partition the room with a wire screen. In one half I left the dingo, in the other, Perry, and then I went away. But I came back several times before finally leaving, and peeped in at the window.

When it found itself quite alone the puppy felt miserable. It was cold without its mother, and lonely. It began whining. I could see Perry was upset. Whether the whining of the puppy reminded her of her own babies, or whether her maternal instincts were aroused, I cannot say, but she got up several times, pattered over to the partition and tried to lick the puppy through the wire netting. Next morning Perry was not in her place. She was lying next to the bars, and on the other side, pressed against her, slept the puppy.

After this I put them together without the slightest misgivings. The puppy instantly made for Perry. It had got very hungry in the night, and it bumped its nose into her, wagging its tail and whining softly. And Perry made no resistance. She lay down, and the pup, trembling with excitement and shifting its paws, sucked greedily. I felt quite happy about them now. Perry had adopted the pup and there was no need to worry about it any more. We called the pup Chuzhoi (Stranger).

Perry looked after the puppy better than its mother had, and she had more milk. The puppy began to put on flesh. It cheered up, its eyes didn't water any more, its sides rounded out. The jolly, playful pup was not in the least like the former pitiful little creature. It was all over the place, poking its nose into everything. Nothing was safe from it—once it got on to a table and tore up a notebook. I took away the book, and the next time Chuzhoi knocked over an ink bottle. You should have seen him! I did not recognize him at first—the yellow puppy was now quite black. It took me ages to wash off the ink. Chuzhoi sat in a basin, whining, and Perry ran round and round in a state of considerable excitement, quite unable to understand what

was going on. She was always very much upset if anyone touched the pup. She didn't mind people she was used to, but if anyone else came near she was sure to snap. One day a man came to repair the electricity. He got on a ladder, and there the poor fellow had to stay till I came back.

And yet the strange puppy was not quite the same as her own for Perry. In the spring, when the snow began to melt and there were rivulets everywhere, she happened upon the snow-drift in which her puppies had been buried. The drift had blackened and settled, and on the top of it lay the little corpses. It is hard to say whether Perry recognized them, or remembered their smell, but she picked one up in her teeth and carried it home. Then she went back for the rest, one by one, till she had them all. After this she lay down in her corner, placed them in a row, licked them, tried to warm them with her body, and thrust them beneath her nipples. But the little bodies remained cold and still. I tried to take them away but Perry would not let me. She was always very obedient, and she only flattened her ears and looked apologetically into my eyes. I had to take the puppies away by force. Perry lunged after them whining piteously. She would not even eat that day, and when Chuzhoi came up to her she growled angrily and turned from him. After all he was not hers.

Chuzhoi did not take offence. He was a remarkably independent puppy. When I let him out for a walk he did not run after me as puppies of his age usually do. On the contrary, *I* had to run after *him*. He went wherever he liked, did whatever he liked, took no notice when I called him, was always sniffing and seeking. His sense of smell was excellent. Somewhere or other, deep under the snow, he would suddenly dig up the head of a herring, or an old bone, and invariably carried it home. He hid all sorts of rubbish in his straw and guarded it as a treasure.

Chuzhoi was very fond of scaring other animals. On a hill beside the elephant house lived some Siberian goats. They are quite like ordinary goats, only bigger, and they are always grey. When I passed their enclosure with Chuzhoi they would run along inside the railings, and threaten him with their long, terrible horns. But the puppy was not frightened. He even liked it. It was amusing to watch him teasing them and trying to make them come closer. He would lower himself on to his front paws and spring backwards, or, pretending to be frightened, run away, and when the goats were taken in and came quite near the bars, he would rush at them, snapping. He was very pleased if he could get a nip at an unwary animal.

He once attacked a kid, but the kid turned out to be very courageous. It did not take fright, or run away. It reared, balanced on its hind legs for a moment, and suddenly, with a pretty toss of its head, butted the puppy with its horns. Chuzhoi squealed and retreated. The horns were small but very sharp. Chuzhoi ran back to me, his tail tucked between his legs. Ever since, he never attempted to tease goats. The very sight of them alarmed him and he gave them a wide berth when he had to pass their cage.

By the end of May the clumsy, lop-eared puppy had grown into a handsome slender dog with upright ears, like a wolf's, and a smooth yellowish coat. He no longer fed on Perry's milk but they were still good friends. In human beings, however (especially men), Chuzhoi no longer felt the same confidence. He would back away from their advances, snarling—possibly because he had always lived among women. He did not go out for walks often now. Formerly I had let him and Perry out by themselves, but now I was afraid. And I had no time for taking him out on a leash.

The merry, playful dog pined. To while away his boredom he gnawed at chairs and tables and clawed at the walls. So Chuzhoi and Perry had to be moved to the New Territory.

A room in a little wooden house was cleared for the dogs. They had a good time there, running about everywhere, and sometimes looking into the place in which food was prepared. Chuzhoi behaved atrociously, putting his paws on the table, stealing whatever he could find, even if it were only a lump of butter. He had to be driven off with a wet towel.

Chuzhoi and Perry were comically different in their behaviour when out for a walk. Perry strode along slowly, very dignified, but Chuzhoi would rush about the lawns and flower beds, digging holes in the ground, wallowing in the mud. He would return home dirty and smelly. I often told myself it was time to put him in a cage. But I was sorry for Perry. I was afraid that, having lived together so long, they would miss each other and find separation hard to bear. I had forgotten that they were not related to each other.

Separation came of itself and quite unexpectedly. The dingoes were put in an empty enclosure not far from where Perry and Chuzhoi lived. They were Chuzhoi's brothers and sisters. When I let him and Perry out for a walk the dingoes were gambolling about their enclosure. At the sight of his brothers Chuzhoi stood on the alert. He looked at them long and attentively. Then he turned to Perry, as if asking her to go with him, poking at her playfully with his nose. But Perry did not go. Several times Chuzhoi ran off and came back, as if unable to make up his mind. Then all of a sudden he ran over to the dingoes as fast as he could. Perry remained alone. She looked after him for some time, then turned and walked slowly home. Her role as foster-mother was over.

TYULKA

I N THE SUMMER OF 1932, two hyenas were sent to the Moscow Zoo
from southern Turkmenia. I had long been interested in hyenas.
I had read that they were bad-tempered, stupid animals, very hard
to tame, and I was longing to find out if this were true.

Tyulka and Rebecca were sisters—five-month-old, striped hyenas,
queer and clumsy, with heavy, swollen-looking heads. As a rule, young
animals get used to new surroundings sooner than grown-up ones.
They are not so timid, not so afraid of human beings, and a great deal
easier to tame.

And the hyenas soon became fond of me. The moment I came into
the cage they would run to meet me, getting under my feet and utter-

ing the strangest cries, very loud, a sort of creaking note, ending in a long-drawn snore. It was hard to know whether they indicated displeasure or affection, because the hyenas showed both in almost the same way. Tyulka was the one I took the most notice of, stroking her more often than the other, and bringing her sweets. When she was quite used to me I began taking her out for walks. The first time she went out she was terrified at everything—unfamiliar people and animals, and most of all the chain.

It rattled close to her ear, choked her, prevented her from escaping. In her terror Tyulka tried to get away and began biting at everything—the chain, the bench, her own paws. She seemed to have gone mad.

After a struggle I got her by the scruff of her neck and took her back to the cage.

The next time, I used a strap instead of a chain and took her out with Rebecca. Things went better when there were two of them. The sisters pressed close together, and were not quite so frightened.

I let them play in an enclosure. Tyulka was much more playful than Rebecca, she would drag her sister about by the neck, or come up from behind and nibble at her gently. Rebecca was in a continual state of fear, and was always hiding. Tyulka was much braver. Soon she got quite used to going out, and walked freely between the cages, not in the least shy of the visitors.

She went well on the leash but was very stubborn. When she did not want to go on she would stand still or lie down. You could call her, tempt her, tug at her leash, but Tyulka would choke and snort, and still would not budge. She would dig all her four paws into the ground so that it was hard to move her from the spot. I had to pick her up and carry her a little way. This happened very often and soon Tyulka grew so accustomed to this means of progress that she did not even resist. Altogether she allowed me to take all sorts of liberties with her.

She would fight with Rebecca for a piece of meat, but she always gave up her portion to me without so much as a snarl. Sometimes I squeezed a bit of meat in my hand and offered it to Tyulka. She would lick my hand all over, take it right into her mouth, and those teeth which could crush up bones as if they were sugar never left the slightest scratch on my hands.

When the summer came to an end we had to part. Rebecca was sold to another Zoo and Tyulka was transferred to the Animal Islet.

The Animal Islet is on the New Territory and I never had time to go there.

Over a year passed. All that time I never once went to see Tyulka. At first I was afraid of upsetting her, and afterwards I felt sure she **must have forgotten me. But the hyena's memory was** better than I had expected.

At that time I was working as a guide. One day I went into the

lion house and suddenly I heard a snort, a familiar creaky snort, and saw a hyena rushing up and down its cage. It was looking at me. Even the visitors noticed this. For a long time I could not understand what it was all about.

It was a full-grown hyena that I did not

seem to know, and yet it was making loving advances and snorting to me. Afterwards I learned from the attendant that this was Tyulka and that she had been temporarily transferred to the lion house.

I went to see her several times after this and petted her, and then I went away for my holidays. I came back in two months. I was told that Tyulka was being transferred that very day to the Animal Islet, where the other hyenas were, and I went to have a look.

Boy and Girl were much bigger hyenas than Tyulka. They had grown up together and did not give the newcomer a friendly welcome. Their fur stood on end and they went round and round Tyulka, snorting fiercely.

Poor Tyulka was huddled up in the farthest corner, uttering plaintive cries. The first to bite her was Girl. When Tyulka turned round, Boy bit her. It took a long time to drive them away from Tyulka. The attendants tried to get her out, but Tyulka, mad with pain and fear, would not let anyone come near her. She attacked the attendants and snatched the sticks out of their hands, grinding them into little bits with her teeth. An attempt was made to get a net over her, but this, too, was a failure.

Then I decided to get her out myself. Everybody tried to dissuade me. They said nothing would come of it, that she had been separated from me too long, and would not recognize me. But I went in just the same.

When she saw me, Tyulka pressed still close to the wall, growling and glaring at me with eyes full of rage. Her fur stood on end, making her seem bigger, and her blood-smeared muzzle and the gaping wound on her neck gave her an unusually savage look.

To tell the truth, I did not feel quite at my ease. I made several attempts to approach her but each time she rushed at me, snapping.

Then I asked everyone to go out of the enclosure, and, moving a little way off, began calling to her.

"Tyulka, little one," I coaxed. "Come to me, Fatty!"

Whether it was the familiar words and voice, or whether she simply recognized me, I don't know, but Tyulka, terrible, blood-smeared Tyulka, a full-grown hyena, suddenly snorted, ran up to me and began rubbing against my dress, leaving traces of blood all over it, crawling at my feet and lying flat on her belly.

I put a collar on her neck, right under her ears for fear of touching her wound, and led her out. We had to go all round the Animal Islet and a little way inside a building. We had not been out together for a very long time, she might have taken fright, run away; worse still, she might have tugged at the leash, hurting herself, and turning savage. But none of these things happened.

The collar slipped low on her neck, right over her wound, but Tyulka did not seem to notice the pain.

She followed me quietly as if we had been going out for walks every day. Then she allowed me to pick her up, put her in the cage and take off the collar.

She lived a long time in the Zoo, and although I very seldom found the time to go and see her, as soon as she heard my voice she would begin to cry out and run up and down her cage, asking to be petted, and when I went away she would stand for a long time rubbing herself against the bars through which I had stretched my hands to her.

LOSKA

FIRST ACQUAINTANCE

EVERYTHING went wrong from the very morning. The milk turned, the meat did not come in time. The hungry Zoo babies squealed in a medley of voices, and that was the moment chosen for a baby moose to be brought to us. I had brought up wolf cubs, fox cubs, baby otters and all sorts of other beasties, but I had never had charge of a baby moose before, and I did not know how to begin. It was a little yellowish creature rather like a calf, with long ears like a donkey's, and a long muzzle—very unfamiliar indeed. I put it into a pen.

It was a big, comfortable pen with a little house for shelter if it rained. My first acquaintance with the baby moose was not a success. The moment I came into the pen he pricked up his big, sensitive ears and ran away. I called to him, tried to tempt him with milk, but he only ran away. I could not persuade him to come to me. I had to put off the acquaintance for another time.

The next day my new charge, who had had time during the night to work up a good appetite, was not so refractory. The smell of warm milk made him still hungrier. He came up to me squealing plaintively, but did not venture to take the rubber nipple. Then I squatted down, stretched out my hand with the bottle in it, and kept very still. As a rule this works—a human being seems smaller and the animal approaches more boldly. And that is what the baby moose did. He minced up cautiously, on the tips of his hoofs, craning his neck comically. He sniffed at the nipple, licked it, and suddenly, taking almost the whole of the neck of the bottle into his mouth, began sucking with evident enjoyment. The bottle was frothy with bubbles, and although I had long ago got to my feet, the moose drank and drank.

At the next feeding he came up more boldly. He let me stroke the tip of his muzzle, and by the end of the day ran up to me of his own accord.

FRIENDS

Loska (Moosie), as I called the moose, made friends with me very quickly. In a few days he was following me about as if I were his mother, and pined when I left him, roaming his pen disconsolately with long-drawn wails, looking all the time in the direction from which I usually came. Loska's sight was poor. If I wore a dress he had not seen before, he had to look and sniff a long time to make sure it was really me. But his hearing and sense of smell were very keen. The moment he heard my voice in the distance he rushed to meet me. He had very affectionate ways, and would put his head on my shoulder, nipping my cheek delicately with his lips. When he did this I loved him as I have never loved any other animal.

A day never passed without my coming to see my pet and bringing him some little treat. I shared my breakfast and dinner with him. He would eat anything—sweets, sugar, pies, and even sandwiches. In a word, there was nothing he would not take from my hands.

He was ill once, I remember, and refused to take his medicine. The medicine was worked up with bread crumbs into a pellet and soaked in milk, but the moose's sense of smell was too good to be so easily taken in. Then I undertook to give him the medicine. I made no attempt to conceal it or smother the taste, I just poured it on to a piece of bread and coaxed Loska to eat it. He held out for a long time, sniffing, snorting, and turning his head away. Several times he took it in his mouth and spat it out again. But in the end he swallowed it. And yet he would not even take food from a stranger. Perhaps this was because I always prepared his food myself, choosing it to suit his taste. Not everyone knew what he liked. When he was little he was very fond of carrots and rusks, but later on he acquired a taste for oats, bran mash and bread. He would not touch hay, but liked the branches of asps and oaks. By the end of the winter these were usually scarce, but there was always some for Loska.

LOSKA IN TROUBLE

Loska was very particular about food, often picking out the dainti-est bits and scattering the rest on the ground. I had endless quarrels with him about this. He was really too spoiled. What if acorns are bitter—they're nourishing, aren't they?

So to punish him I would not take him for his walk. And Loska was very fond of his walks. He would eat the nastiest and bitterest food if only I would take him out. We went for walks early in the morning before visitors came. We walked all over the grounds of the Zoo, sometimes going for provisions to the housekeeping department, or even into the buffet. Loska had his favourite places, but there were some he was afraid of and always avoided when possible. Usually there was some reason for this. He was afraid of the lion house, for instance, having once had a fright there. He strayed in casual-ly, through the open door. And what excitement and noise were caused by his appearance! The leopards dashed at the bars of their cages, the lions strode up and down roaring, and Radji, the most ferocious of the tigers, crouched silently, waiting for the moment to spring.

Poor Loska! He was so terrified that he tried to get out by the wrong door. I took him back to the right one. He pressed against me, trembling all over.

Ever after, Loska knew the lion house very well and squinted and laid back his ears timidly when we passed it. But he never missed the buffet. He knew very well what awaited him there. Picking his way soberly amongst the tables he would go up to the counter. The girl there knew him. When she gave him the dainties I had paid for she would add something on her own account, and Loska would walk away solemnly.

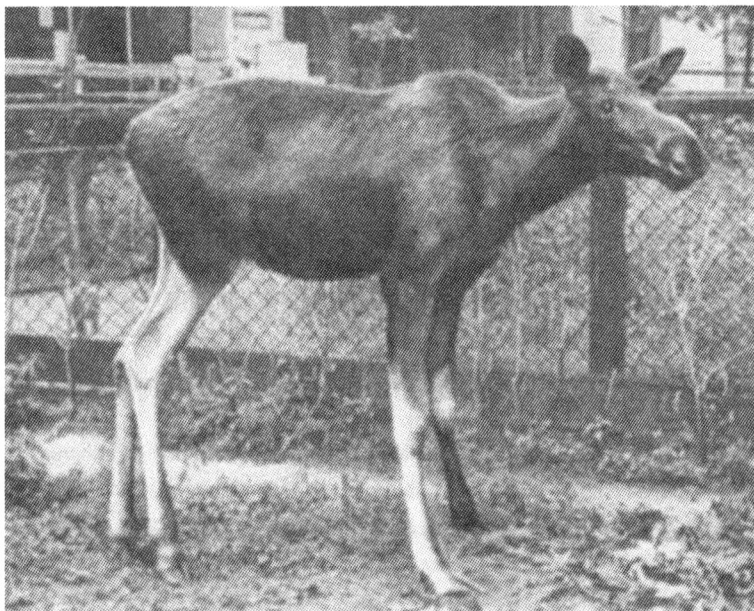

But his favourite walk of all was the path round the big pond in the Zoo. He enjoyed running about and gambolling there and, most of all, nibbling the tasty branches of the willows. How he loved them! More than carrots, more than rusks, even more than sugar.

Sometimes he enjoyed this feast so much that, though usually so obedient, he did not come at once when I called him. Not for nothing did everyone call him a sweet-tooth. At first I took no notice of this, but when it began to happen too often I decided to teach the disobedient moose a lesson the next time we went for a walk round the pond.

While Loska was busy with his willow branches, I slipped quietly away and hid in the bushes. "Well!" thought I. "Try and find me! That'll teach you to be disobedient!" I waited and wondered what would happen.

Loska did not at once notice that I had gone. But how frightened he was when he found himself alone! He dashed forward with the cry mooses use for calling their mothers. He galloped so furiously that it seemed as if nothing could stop him. I was terrified. Supposing he were to stumble, and break a leg!

"Loska, Loska!" I shouted, springing out of my ambush.

At the first sound of my voice Loska stood stock-still. Then he came back to me and kept very close to me the whole way, as if afraid of losing himself again.

MY PROTECTOR

In the summer I began storing up dry branches for Loska to eat during the winter. I chose the best in the storehouse and put them away in Loska's house. Loska was so big now that he could hardly get into it. In the autumn he turned grey and his long legs were white.

Loska was mistrustful of strangers and would not allow himself to be touched. But I could do whatever I liked with him. Once, when he ran a nail into his hoof, he would allow no one else to wash the wound. And how carefully would he let himself down beside me in his cramped dwelling if I stayed to sit with him a while. Before taking a step he would feel for a long time with his hoof, for fear of treading on me, trembling from the uncomfortable pose and the tenseness of his muscles.

While he was still quite a little moose he would try to defend me, laying back his ears, squinting and stamping his slender hoofs angrily. This amused me so much that I sometimes asked one of the attendants to shout at me, or make threatening gestures. At first everyone was willing to tease him, but when Loska grew from a little yellow calf to a half-grown grey moose, there were fewer and fewer volunteers. And at last nobody dared to come near me in his presence. And not without reason. . . .

One day, while walking about the Zoo with Loska, I met a watchman. He was new to the Zoo, having only recently been taken on. He did not know that Loska was allowed to browse on the branches, and began scolding me for allowing him to spoil the trees. I tried to explain to him that Loska had permission, but he shouted so loudly that he could not hear what I was saying. When Loska heard the noise he stopped eating and gazed attentively at the wildly gesticulating watchman, and then, flattening his ears and stepping high with his front feet, slowly advanced upon him. Loska was very terrible. Even I was afraid of him at that moment. His eyes were bloodshot and his fur stood on end, so that he looked much bigger than usual. The watchman, too, took fright.

Not far from the place where we were standing was the monkey house. The watchman fled to it and hardly had time to slam the door behind him when Loska reared on to his hind legs, and struck at the door with his two sharp front hoofs, which left their deep imprint on the wood. After this people feared him more than ever, and no wonder!

JEALOUSY

Loska was very jealous. If I stroked another animal in front of him he got very cross and tried to kick it.

I had many four-footed friends in the Zoo. When I took Loska out for walks I would now and again go up and stroke one or other of them, and sometimes I went to visit my tame wolf. After the incident in the lion house Loska feared wild animals, but jealousy was stronger than fear. He would dash at the cage, get on to his hind legs and bang against the bars with his front hoofs. And there they were—on one side the wolf, on the other, the moose, trying to get at one another.

In the autumn another baby moose was brought to the Zoo. Its name was Vaska.

Vaska was tame and was put in with Loska for company.

But the two mooses did not make friends, either the first, or succeeding days. They ate from different mangers, kept to different parts of the pen. One might have thought they had quarrelled, so strictly did they stick to their own sides. This was Loska's doing, and all because I paid more attention to Vaska. Before Vaska's arrival I had only had Loska to pet, and I could see that it made him very cross to have a rival in the pen.

Vaska made several overtures to Loska, going towards him and craning his neck in friendly fashion, but Loska was adamant, and every day his enmity increased.

One day I went into the pen. Vaska ran after me and accidentally overstepped the invisible line dividing their pen.

Loska was on him like a hurricane, knocking him down, and striking out at him with his hoofs. Vaska lay on the ground at if stunned. I tried in vain to defend him, and neither the shouts nor the blows of the watchman who ran up to my aid had any effect. Loska was too furious to heed them. At last Vaska managed to struggle to his feet. Pursued by Loska, he fled. Poor Vaska was so overcome that he made no attempt at self-defence, merely trying to avoid the blows and uttering piteous cries. Either because of these cries, or because he was tired of the whole thing, once Loska had driven Vaska into the house, he left him alone. After this he kept him in perpetual terror, monopolizing both the mangers and the whole pen, only allowing Vaska to eat by fits and starts, and constantly kicking him. When the weather was bad Loska turned Vaska out of the house, when it was fine he drove him into it.

172

Poor Vaska! Cowed by Loska, he did not even put up a fight, but submitted to him in everything, and yet he was always getting into trouble, especially if he ventured to approach me. It came to such a pass that at sight of me Vaska would immediately run away.

By the autumn Loska had grown very big. Now he could easily jump the hedge round the pen and had to be transferred to a larger one.

His new home was much better. There were plenty of trees and grass, and lots of space for play and exercise. The only thing wrong with it was that it was at the other end of the Zoo and I could not go there often. Loska did not like this. He was accustomed to see me all day and he obviously missed my company.

And how glad he was to see me! He would follow we about, rubbing his face against me and, as before, nipping at my cheeks softly with his lips. Sometimes he would start a game. He would find an "enemy"—a chip, a clod, or a twig—throw himself upon it, kick it, trample it underfoot or—he would begin to lope round and round the pen. Loska usually played like this in the mornings, when there was nobody there to interfere with him. The rest of the day he lay down, or strolled about the pen.

THE END

Autumn drew to a close, winter came. That winter my little son fell ill. I got leave of absence from work and stayed at home. Loska, not seeing me as usual, showed signs of dejection. He walked about the pen uttering loud cries. A few days later I got a telephone call saying that he would not eat.

I went to the Zoo. Loska knew me by the crunching of the snow under my feet. He sprang up and ran swiftly to meet me, and then to the manger, where he ate long and voraciously. After a while I stole away very quietly, so that he should not notice. Turning for a last look, I caught sight of Loska, plunging up to the bars, and his prolonged cries pursued me on my way.

Now began my worries. At home—a sick child, in the Zoo—Loska, who would not take his food unless I was there. Whenever I went to him, he would first dash up to me, and then to the manger. He only walked in the part of the pen from which he had caught sight of me the last time. A deep hollow in the snow showed that he slept there, too, while the untrampled snow and the beaten path across it showed that he never went anywhere else, not even to his manger, around which the freshly-fallen snow lay smooth and untrodden.

Loska began to starve. His sides fell in, his smooth fur was shaggy, and he was nothing but skin and bone.

He grew worse and worse every day. The hollow in which he lay became deeper and deeper from the weight of his body and the tracks on the path were fewer.

At last the day came when Loska could hardly get up, and swayed on his feeble legs. His hoofs sank into the deep snow, he lifted them out with an effort, and when he put them down again his legs shook. He no longer went to his manger. After long coaxing he took a few bits of dry bread, chewed and spat out the sweet I gave him, touched my cheek with his lips, and again lay down.

All that night I could not sleep. I kept seeing Loska—sometimes well and jolly, sometimes as I had last seen him.

I got up very early. I felt intolerably uneasy, and could do nothing properly. Everything seemed mournful and oppressive. As soon as possible I hastened to the Zoo.

174

But there was no Loska any more. No one came to meet me, no one got up on my arrival.

The snow had covered up all tracks, only in the place where Loska had lain there was still a hollow.

It is many years since Loska died. All sorts of young animals have passed through my hands since then, but I still cannot forget the little yellow calf we called Loska.

ARGO

WHEN I WENT into the cage the wolf cub backed into a corner, squinting in its terror. I liked him at once, with his yellowish fur and his round forehead. I liked him all the more for gnashing his teeth and leaping away when I approached.

That's the sort of wolf cub I like. They are difficult to tame, but once they get fond of one they never forget their master.

I called the wolf cub Argo. I went to see him every day, bringing him bones and scraps of meat, but Argo would not touch them, and was as wild as ever. It was ten days before he would take a bit of meat from my hands. And then, with timid side-glances at me, he ate it up and retired to his corner again. It took me a lot of trouble and patience to get him to allow me to stroke him. At first he seemed to be petrified, hiding his nose between his paws and lying perfectly still, staring in front of him fixedly. While putting up with my petting he never invited it. But I shall never forget my joy when he first showed affection for me.

It was quite a surprise. I had been away from the Zoo about two weeks. The first thing I did when I got back was to go and see my latest nursling. I was afraid the separation would have made him still wilder, that he would have forgotten me, and would not let me touch him again. But nothing of the sort! The moment I opened the door and came into the building, the wolf cub rushed up to meet me at the bars of his cage. I could hardly believe my eyes when I saw him wagging his tail, whining, and trying to get at me.

I even thought I must have made a mistake, though I knew Argo very well.

In the next cage was Lobo, another wolf cub, who was quite tame, and I decided that it must be him. I took a look at both cages—no, Lobo was in his place, and Argo, savage little Argo, was unrecognizable, crawling on his belly, as glad to see me as if he had been tame all his life.

From that moment everything went well and I was soon taking Argo out on a leash. Of course this took a little time. At first he was terrified, pressed against my legs, tugged at the leash, or, suddenly taking fright, rushed back. But that was only at the beginning. Argo showed himself an apt pupil and was soon walking on the leash as well as a dog.

In the summer he was put into Lobo's cage. The cubs, though of very different dispositions, became firm friends. If one was taken out

the other felt lonely and strained after his comrade. They were usually taken out together.

A friend of mine would take Lobo and I would take Argo and we would walk about the paths of the Zoo. Sometimes, if there was no one in the Zoo, we let the cubs off the leash. They would gambol and chase one another exactly like puppies. They did not go far from us. Argo, more independent, sometimes went a little farther away, but I only had to pretend to be going back, and he would return at once.

ARGO GROWS UP

Thanks to frequent walks and good care, Argo developed very well. He grew a lot in the summer, till he was the size of a big dog, and by the end of the winter he was fully matured. He was now a strong, dangerous wolf. But he was only dangerous for others, for me he was always the little cub Argo. I could do anything I liked with him, rumple his fluffy fur, pull him by his paws or his tail. And never once did he snap at me.

Once Argo got eczema. This is not a dangerous disease, but it is very distressing. In the space of a month or so Argo's dense fluffy fur came out and his body, inflamed by the disease, was covered with sores. They had to be smeared with salve. I looked after this. The ointment stung badly. When I rubbed it into his skin Argo would lie on his back from the pain, whining and catching at my hands with his lips, his inch-long fangs lightly closed, never causing me the slightest pain.

This does not mean that Argo could not bite. His teeth could easily crunch up bones and there were other things as well as meat that his fangs could rend.

A dog attacked him that winter, a big dog, much bigger than Argo, whom it probably took for an Alsatian. When the dog got nearer, it suddenly realized that Argo was a wolf and turned and fled, but it was too late—Argo was after it in a trice. The dog fled in terrified bounds, floundering in the snow, and staggering out again. Argo pursued it with his long measured stride. I shouted at him in vain. He was so absorbed that he seemed to hear nothing. He drew nearer and nearer, now he was on the dog's heels, now he had caught up with it. The dog rolled to one side, its neck torn open to the shoulder, and Argo, the half-grown wolf, returned without a single scratch.

THE WOLF'S HATRED

Argo would not go up to strangers, but so long as they did not touch him he let them alone, behaving as if he did not notice them.

One day I let Argo into the pen for a run and went away. Returning in half an hour I found the gate of the pen ajar and no wolf there.

I was frightened—suppose he were to get up to mischief, to bite someone. ... It was a Sunday and the Zoo was full of visitors. I ran about looking for the truant, and I at last found him next to the eagles' cage. He was walking amongst the crowd, looking round and behaving so quietly that nobody realized he was a wolf.

It was a good thing Argo did not come across Nikolai Mikhailovich, an employee at the veterinary station whom he did not like, whom, in fact, he hated, and for the most trivial reason. Argo was once taken ill, and Nikolai Mikhailovich, who had to transfer him to another cage, bound a cord round his jaws to prevent him from biting. For this act of violence Argo detested him. Wolves have good memories, and six months later Argo almost managed to revenge himself on Nikolai Mikhailovich. This is how it happened.

A yak escaped from its pen. Nikolai Mikhailovich and some other Zoo employees went after it. They had to pass Argo, who had lately been kept chained to a kennel. When he caught sight amongst the pursuers of the man he hated, Argo did not jump at him. He crouched behind his kennel, watching him as a cat watches a mouse. Nikolai Mikhailovich had quite forgotten that there might be danger for him, and began passing quite close to the wolf.

Every time he passed, Argo's grey body twitched and he started almost imperceptibly, but he always settled down again.

Argo was only too well aware of the limits of his chain. Very often, sitting chained up all day, he amused himself by catching sparrows, becoming quite an adept, and never missing one. He knew the range beyond which he could not get at them, and never made a mistake. He made no mistake this time, either.

And the moment Nikolai Mikhailovich came within this range Argo was on him in a single powerful bound.

Nikolai Mikhailovich was saved by the merest chance. Argo had tugged so violently at his chain that he was thrown back. He recovered his balance immediately and made another forward lunge, but Nikolai Mikhailovich was already in safety, fingering the torn collar of his shirt. . . .

A NEW HOME

After this, Argo, Lobo, and a she-wolf called Dikarka, were transferred to the Animal Islet. The Animal Islet was quite different from the cramped dark cages in the old territory. Here were spacious runs, sunlight, grass, trees, and, instead of iron bars, a board moat filled with water. All this created an atmosphere of liberty.

The morose and powerful Argo assumed the lead over the wolves transferred to the Animal Islet with him.

No other wolf must come up to me, or take the first piece of meat. He was the leader of this tiny wolf pack on this tiny plot of ground, which had its own law of liberty.

Wolf cubs born here acquired an extremely curious attitude to me.

They were quite wild, acknowledging nobody's authority, and it was dangerous to approach them empty-handed. Thanks to Argo, however, I could move among them freely. He would not let any of them come up to me, and if one came too near would fall on him and bite him.

ARGO BECOMES A FILM STAR

Argo was the handsomest and strongest of all the wolves. When a wolf was required for a film he was always the first to be chosen.

His first acquaintance with a cinema camera took place in the winter, on the Zoo pond.

A wolf-hunt had to be filmed. The pond was surrounded with flagged cords, to make a snare for the wolves, as in a real wolf-hunt. Wolves are afraid of flags, so much so that they do not even dare to jump over them and escape. Hunters profit by this and shoot at the wolves when the beaters have driven them into the snare.

When all the preparations were completed and the cameraman was posted in a safe place, I went for Argo. He heard the jingling of the chain from a distance and pricked up his ears, whining in his impatience. I fastened the chain, and Argo, wagging his tail, accompanied me cheerfully.

We came to the pond. I let him off the chain and moved away. Argo, wagging his tail joyfully, ran a little way off and then, dropping on to his front paws, began inviting me to play with him. Suddenly the rattling of the camera was heard. The unfamiliar sound immediately attracted the wolf's attention.

He jumped back, on the alert at once, and began anxiously sniffing the air, laying back first one, then the other ear. It was a wonderful sight: the powerful grey body of the wolf was sharply silhouetted against the white snow, as he took a few tense, cautious steps, ready at any moment to leap back or attack. It was exactly what was wanted for the film.

Later in the film the wolf had to be shown at the moment when he came right up to the flags, but did not dare to jump over them. But Argo stubbornly refused to go up to the flags. Try as I might to drive him away, he would not leave my side. I had to find some way of overcoming his obstinacy. I stepped across the cord, went a little farther away and called to Argo.

And suddenly the unexpected occurred. Argo took a running jump, like a dog, soared over the line that no wolf dared to cross, and scampered after me. All the laws of hunting were flaunted. The cameraman's horror-stricken face showed from behind his camera. The shot had been spoilt. It had to be taken all over again.

Then I began walking along the cord, clapping my hands. Argo kept running up to me and jumping back again. This was just what was wanted. The cameraman was delighted and declared that the four-legged star was a great deal cleverer than many two-legged ones.

After this Argo was filmed again and again. He soon got used to the sound of the camera and, taking no more notice of it, did everything required of him. But he regarded the man who cranked the camera as his worst enemy. He was forever trying to wreak his vengeance on the trousers of cameramen, who frequently had to escape from those inch-long fangs by climbing a tree.

I had to act as "interpreter" for the star. The producer told me the "business" required from the wolf, and I thought out ways of getting him to do it. This was not very hard, since I thoroughly understood Argo's character. But once during the shooting of a film there was an incident that almost ended badly.

A fight between a woman and a wolf had to be filmed. This was not in itself difficult. Argo loved playing and during a game would often rush at me, pretending to bite me. All that was required was to get him to play.

We arrived at the place chosen. The producer, who had never had anything to do with wild animals before, thought the wolf could wait, and busied himself over something else. It was getting on for three o'clock, Argo's usual time for receiving his meat ration, and hunger made him get more and more restless. He kept lying down and getting up again. Seeing this I insisted that the shooting should begin immediately.

At last everything was ready. My face was made up and I was told to put on a sheepskin coat. I objected to the coat, which had a strong smell of sheep, a great temptation for a hungry wolf. But there was no arguing with them, and no time, anyhow. I went up to the prowling wolf. Argo rushed at me with lightning speed, sinking his steely teeth into the sheepskin. His eyes glowed wrathfully and his fur stood on end. I had to call him several times by his name as calmly as possible before my familiar voice reached the wolf's consciousness. Argo slowly and reluctantly unclenched his teeth, gazing long and steadily into my face. At last, recognizing me, he laid back his ears apologetically, and gave himself a shake. His fur smoothed down, and it was hard to believe that only a minute before I had been confronted by an infuriated wild beast.

Argo was filmed many a time in numbers of pictures—"Wolf-Hunt," "The Skotinins," "The Battle of Life," and others.

He is old now, his teeth are blunted, he has lost his inch-long fangs. Younger wolves are ready to take his place, but Argo is still the handsomest wolf on the Animal Islet—Argo, the film star.

A BROWNIE IN THE ZOO

WHEN ZOO ATTENDANT Pravikov went to clean the lion house one morning he did not recognize the place. The floor was littered with broken flowerpots, flowers and earth, and the ashes had been raked from the open stove. Pravikov rubbed his eyes. He and Pavel, the assistant attendant, had left everything in order the night before, and now!... Who could have done it? But there was no time for speculation. The place had to be cleaned and the cages washed before visitors started coming. Just then Pavel came in, and the attendants, having come to the conclusion that it must be a practical joke, started on their job. Pravikov began with the huge tiger Radji, as usual. Radji was the most ferocious tiger in the Zoo. When Pravikov came up to him he used to dash against the bars, striking them so violently with his paws that the cage shook.

Pravikov was not afraid of Radji. He knew the tiger's paw was too broad to squeeze between the bars, and that the narrow paw of Vaska, the leopard, was much more to be feared. Vaska liked to hunt, even in the cage. When Pravikov went past he would crouch in a corner and watch him—exactly like a cat watching a mouse. And if the attendant was off his guard for an instant, out came Vaska's paw—a powerful paw with sharp claws, from which it was hard to escape once they had you.

The attendant knew his animals well. He wondered why Vaska did not throw himself against the bars as usual. When Pravikov got nearer, he saw blood in the leopard's cage, and there were stains of blood all over the floor. Pravikov was alarmed. He snatched up a long iron rod and started banging on the bars. The animal had to be made to get up, so that Pravikov could see what was the matter with it. Vaska got up and limped away a step or two. One of his front paws left a bloody trail.

The vet was sent for. He coaxed Vaska up to the bars, took a good look at his paw, and said it had been bitten. Although the leopard Maruska who shared Vaska's cage never bit, suspicion fell upon her.

The rest of the day passed as usual. At two o'clock the meat ration arrived, at three the animals were fed, and the attendants, after filling up the drinking troughs, went home.

The next morning Pravikov and Pavel arrived together. They unlocked the door of the lion house, and stood aghast. What could have happened? You might have thought they had not cleaned up the place yesterday. Everywhere lay potsherds and broken plants, and Maruska, Pravikov's favourite, had a bleeding paw. This was too much!

Leaving everything as they had found it, the attendants went to ask the night watchman whether anyone had taken the key of the lion house. The watchman was quite offended. "In all the years I've been working here," he shouted, "nothing has ever gone wrong!"

The vet, after examining Maruska's paw, said that this was a bite, too.

Exactly the same sort of bite was found on the front paw of one of the panthers.

From this day the attendants had no peace. Every morning when they unlocked the lion house they found it in a mess, every morning one of the animals was bitten. Pravikov did not know what to think. He tried everything. He took the key with him, made marks on the door, but all to no purpose. As for Pavel, he had been quite certain all along that this was the work of a brownie. He firmly believed in witches and devils and, having come to the conclusion that the Evil One had established himself in the lion house, applied to be transferred. It was then decided to discover the cause of these nocturnal events, and catch the brownie.

That evening, when Pravikov and Pavel gave up their keys and went home, some boys from the Young Biologists' Club approached the night watchman, asking him for the keys of the lion house and showing him a note from the manager. The watchman was greatly surprised, but gave them the keys. Long after they had gone, he stood looking after them.

Later on, when the Zoo was closed, the boys went to the lion house, where, unlocking the door, they went in and hid under the long row of cages. There was a little bustling about for some time, but soon everything was quiet. The animals, aroused by the intrusion, calmed down, all except Radji, who yearned for freedom, and strode backwards and forwards in his cage for a long time, mewing hoarsely. But at last he, too, lay down. It was perfectly quiet, and the ticking of the clock could be heard. Eleven o'clock struck.

Suddenly a rustling sound came from a far corner of the lion house. The boys started, but were immediately relieved—it was only the badger waking up. He went up to the bars of his cage, sniffed the air and climbed cautiously to the top of the cage. The leopard woke up and was on the alert immediately. Meanwhile the badger, holding on by the cross bar, thrust its snout between two bars, and wriggled out of the cage.

Vaska the leopard strode up to the bars of his cage, and stood stock-still, waiting for the badger to come near. The unsuspecting badger clambered down the outside of the cage and sauntered along the narrow ledge. As it passed the leopard's cage, the watchful beast gave a spring. Its paw shot far out of the cage to catch the badger, but was hastily withdrawn to the accompaniment of a roar of pain.

Blood flowed from the paw, and the badger went on his way with perfect composure. At the end of the ledge he let himself down by a bench on to the ground and scampered up to the plant stands, his long claws scraping against the floor.

The boys longed to catch the truant, but remembering that this was not what they had come for they stayed where they were.

The badger did not notice any danger. It climbed lightly to the top of the stand and began knocking down the pots. The fragile chrysanthemums and asters were broken in the fall.... Their beautiful white blossoms were scattered over the floor and the lion house was filled with the noise of falling pots. The animals woke up, and began striding up and down their cages, roaring, darting furious glances at the rioter, but the badger went on with his business. It went from one plant stand to another, till all the flowers in the lion house were on the floor. Then it began throwing the earth out of the broken pots, searching diligently for something, and munching it up with evident relish when found.

After he had done with the flowers, the badger overturned all the spittoons and stands, even getting into the stove and throwing the ashes on to the floor. Then he began playing. His movements were so funny that the ambushed boys could hardly keep from laughing. The badger, his body as lithe as if there were no bones in it, turned somersaults, his fur standing on end till he looked like a ball. He jumped up and down like a clock-work toy, and then lay on his back, holding a fragment of flowerpot or a pebble between his front paws.

The night passed. A narrow strip of daylight showed through the windows of the lion house. But not one of the boys had slept. You couldn't sleep with a badger around.

There was the sound of keys jingling outside. When he heard this the badger started. Then, with a sudden snort, he ran hastily up to a stool, got on to the ledge and back to his cage by the familiar route, through the opening between the bars under the roof. The cage served him as a burrow and the badger sought shelter in it. Hardly had he disappeared when Pravikov and Pavel came in. At the sight of the disorder in the house, and the boys creeping out from beneath the cages, they could only spread out their hands in astonishment. The boys, shouting one another down, began telling them about the badger's nocturnal antics.

"But we didn't see any brownie," said one of the boys in conclusion.

Pravikov laughed. He went up to the badger's cage, took a good look at the bent bars and carefully wound wire between them. From that day there was perfect order in the lion house, and Pavel stopped believing in brownies.

SHANGO

SHANGO WAS the biggest elephant in the Zoo. Little children used to shout to their mothers: "Look at the mountain, Mummy!" And he really was like a mountain, so big, so heavy, and so grey.

He came to us from a menagerie. We were told that he was very savage and dangerous, and that was why he was sent to the Zoo.

Shango was brought by train on a big railway truck—he was too big to get into a van. The truck was boarded up all round, and a roof and a door made, till it looked just like a house on wheels. And Shango travelled in this house. He was chained to the floor, and his keepers stayed there with him. They watched every movement of the elephant, but this did not prevent him from taking the whole structure to pieces and tossing the fragments on to the rails. But when he got to Moscow Shango behaved perfectly, following the attendant obediently all the way to the Zoo and going as obediently into the place prepared for him.

When I came next morning to have a look at Shango, he was standing in the elephant house, chained by all his four feet. He kept lifting his feet one after another, and touching the chains with his trunk. The chains were big and heavy, it took two men to lift them, but they seemed as light as feathers for this giant.

Shango was not put in with the other elephants. We had to get to know him first, to study his temper, his ways.

At first the elephant behaved very well. So well that we no longer believed the tales of his violent temper.

At the very first signal Shango would seat his keeper carefully on his head, and put him down again just as carefully. When told to lie down he did so at once, although this was very difficult in the cramped house, with his legs chained.

For this docility it was soon decided to put Shango in with the other elephants.

AT LIBERTY

There were four other elephants in the Zoo as well as Shango— Nona, Djindau, Manka and Mirza. The biggest of these was the African elephant Nona, and the smallest was Mirza. Mirza was still quite a young elephant, very fretful and spoilt. The Zoo attendants were particularly anxious on her account—who could say how Shango would treat such a baby? What if he were to strike her with his trunk, perhaps injure her?

But the risk had to be taken. A huge elephant like that could not stand chained to the floor of the elephant house all his life.

When the chains were removed from Shango's feet and the door was opened for him to go out on to Elephant Hill, Shango could not understand what was wanted of him. He stood where he was, shifted from foot to foot, after the age-long habit of chained elephants. He even seemed to miss the familiar clanking of the chains. He felt them with his trunk, lifting them and putting them down again, took a few uncertain steps towards the door, stopped, stood still for a few moments and suddenly, picking up the chains with his trunk, strode firmly into the enclosure.

When they saw Shango the other elephants huddled together and watched him with curiosity. But he strode past them as if noticing nothing, walked to the top of Elephant Hill, and stood there. This is the highest place in the Zoo.

The whole Zoo, with all its cages, ponds and trees, seemed to lie at the feet of this giant. Shango stood there motionless as a statue. A heavy chain dangled from his trunk. The elephant remained quite still for a while and then, suddenly flung the chain far from him. At the clanging sound it made in falling, Shango raised his trunk on high and all the Zoo dwellers heard his trumpet call. At first he trumpeted alone, but soon the other elephants joined in. They circled round him, drumming on the ground with their trunks and trumpeting so loudly, all together, that no other sound could be heard.

From the very first, the elephants accepted Shango as their leader, and yielded to him in everything. Even Mirza, after she had been punished for disobedience, became well-behaved. The elephants came out of their house all together now, Shango leading the way, and neither force nor blandishments could get them out of the house

194

without Shango. In the evening he drove them back, pushing them from behind with his head.

The elephants no longer quarrelled over their food or stole each other's portions, for if any of them did, the culprit immediately got a blow from Shango's trunk.

But from this period Shango's behaviour to human beings changed entirely. The attendants had always approached the elephants fearlessly, giving them their food and cleaning the enclosure at their own convenience. But now Shango began to chase them away. Lifting his trunk he would run straight at a man. The attendants had to invent all sorts of ruses for deceiving Shango before they could get on to Elephant Hill. They would tempt him with food, and clean up while he ate. But this did not work for long. One day Shango noticed the attendant and attacked him as soon as he came nearer. The latter started to run away, but stumbled and fell. The others were rooted

to the spot in terror. Someone cried out. Everyone expected to see the elephant crush the man to death before their very eyes. But Shango did not hurt him. Lifting him gently with his trunk he set him on his feet, only giving him a "gentle" push with his trunk as he climbed over the barrier. But even this gentle push sent the man flying.

Although the elephant had behaved with generosity there were no more volunteers to go near him after this incident.

It was decided to drive Shango inside the elephant house while cleaning was going on outside. He was lured there by food and when he went in the door was promptly shut. Great agility was required to shut the door in time, and this was always done by an experienced keeper who had worked a long time with elephants and knew their ways. Sometimes Shango would get stubborn and refuse to go into the elephant house. Then the keeper would take away his food. Hunger did its work and the elephant had to submit. But Shango marked the man who had incurred his displeasure by locking him into the elephant house, and did not forget him.

THE HATRED OF SHANGO

Shango took a strong dislike to his keeper and did everything he could to vex him, lashing out at him with his trunk and throwing stones at him. There were plenty of stones on Elephant Hill. Shango would choose the biggest, which were the most convenient for him to hold in his trunk, and throw them. True, his aim was not very good and the keeper could dodge them easily enough, and so no one attached any importance to the elephant's behaviour.

But Shango perfected his skill daily. The path along which the keeper came and went was strewn with stones. Shango would watch for his enemy by the hour at the entrance to the elephant house, looking out for him among the visitors. The keeper tried to keep out of Shango's way, especially when the Zoo was open, lest a stone meant for him should strike some visitor. And yet, for all his carefulness, Shango almost killed him. It happened like this: the keeper went to the book-keeper's office, the window of which looked on to Elephant Hill. Everything going on in the office could be seen from Elephant Hill, and Shango caught sight of his enemy in there.

Nobody noticed the elephant pick up a stone and take to the barrier. The keeper was just coming out of the office, when there was a sound of breaking glass behind him and a huge stone whistled over his head and fell on a desk. An inkstand was smashed into smithereens, all the papers were drenched in ink, and stones flew in through the window. The people in the office, protecting their heads with open files, only just managed to run out of the room, while Shango, now thoroughly worked up, went on hurling stones into the room for a long time.

After this it was decided to chain the elephant up again. But Shango wasn't going to allow this. When they separated him from the other elephants he flew into a rage, hurling himself about the elephant house, lashing out with his trunk, roaring, and at last starting to bend the heavy bars of the partition. He thrust his huge tusks between them and we could see a bar give slowly under their pressure. He went on bending the bars till he broke a bit off the end of one tusk. It broke off with a grinding sound and fell, but the elephant went on working at the bars with the other. To prevent Shango breaking his other tusk too we had to let him go back to the other elephants.

There was only one thing left to do—to clear the enclosure of stones. It took ten men several days of hard work to do this. They dug up the earth all over the enclosure, picked out the stones, and sifted the earth to get rid of the smallest pebbles.

But even this did not help. Loaves, beetroot, carrots, potatoes, in fact all the food allotted to Shango and his herd, were thrown by the elephant at the detested keeper. At last the man had to be transferred to other work.

CUNNING SHANGO

After the departure of the man he hated Shango seemed to calm down. He stopped making rows and even began to behave better to the other attendants. Most of the day he basked in the sun, and when it became too hot went to bathe in the pool. Shango loved bathing. He woud wade into the deepest part and swim about, or plunge into the water and disappear from view.

Visitors loved to watch the elephant bathe and there was always a crowd round him at that hour. The cunning animal would fill its trunk with water and use it as a fire-hose to drench the onlookers. Victims rushed away swearing, dirty water streaming down their clothes. Many went to complain to the manager.

There were so many complaints that an attendant had to be posted beside the pool to warn visitors that they might get wet when Shango bathed. Shango seemed to enjoy catching visitors unawares and when he was deprived of this pleasure he invented a new form of amuse-ment—snatching hats and caps from the heads of visitors. And it must be admitted that he did it with extreme agility and craftiness. He actually lured visitors nearer, draping his trunk over the barrier and swinging it slowly from side to side. It looked just like a snake, coiling, straightening itself out, or simply hanging motionless over the barrier. The elephant's drowsy good-natured expression and the motionless trunk resting on the barrier would tempt people to draw nearer. They came right up to the barrier, touched the trunk, took it in their hands. The elephant seemed to be taking no notice, but the moment an uncautious admirer came too close Shango would wave his trunk over the head of the trustful onlooker, whisk off his cap and pop it into his mouth. It was a regular cap-hunt and there were days when Shango ate up quite a number of caps.

He was particularly fond of ladies' hats, especially gaily-coloured ones. Once he caught sight of a most remarkable hat on the head of an elderly lady—it had a wide brim and a big, vividly-tinted flower. The elephant spotted it at once and moved over towards its owner, trying to get her to come closer to the barrier.

Like a salesman obligingly displaying his wares the crafty elephant laid his trunk on the barrier before the confiding lady. If a visitor came between them for a moment Shango blew into his face to make him get out of the way. The elephant's preference for the lady in the hat was so obvious that everyone noticed it. Highly flattered, the lady came quite near and, with the words "What a darling elephant!" stretched out her hand towards him. This was just what the "darling elephant" wanted. He snatched off her hat, and before anyone could intervene, slowly guided it into his mouth.

In vain the lady shouted and threw pebbles at Shango. The broad-brimmed hat with the flower disappeared down the elephant's capacious throat. Shango ate it right up. After this, more attendants had to be put on special duty beside Shango.

ALONE AGAIN

Shango was basking in the sun as usual when the news of war came over the radio. No doubt even the elephant felt that everything was different from that day. In the first place there were hardly any visitors in the Zoo, the familiar male attendants suddenly disappeared, and their places were taken by women.

Trenches were dug all over the grounds of the Zoo.

Then the alerts began.

The shrill wailing notes of the sirens rose above the usual hum of the city. They went on and on in a piercing crescendo till complete silence prevailed in the city, and stopped as suddenly as they had begun.

Shango had never heard the wail of the sirens before. It was not like the howlings of any animal, and it was not like the usual sounds coming from the city. And for some reason it made him uneasy. Everything now seemed to depend on this wail—the fact that the elephants were driven into their house several times a day and that they were sometimes not let out at all.

And once the elephants were left outside their house all night. This time, after the wailing of the sirens, hollow explosions began to shake the earth. The elephants huddled together against the wall of the house, when something suddenly whistled and fell into the enclosure quite near them. It was an incendiary bomb.

It lay there hissing and shooting out liquid fire. The blazing streams showered all round and threatened to set the building on fire.

Shango knew what fire was. In the menagerie he had learned not to touch it, and at the same time not to fear it. But he sensed a foe in this small burning object. A foe against whom he must defend himself, but whom he must not touch. He began instinctively feeling with his trunk for a stone to throw at it, but there were no more stones. Then Shango gathered up some sand in his trunk and sprayed it over the bomb. The flames seemed to shrink. He threw more sand, and more again.... He went on spraying sand till the fire was extinguished and nothing but a little mound was left in the place where the bomb had fallen. Then Shango behaved as his race has always behaved towards its most hated foes—he stood on this mound and trampled it with his feet till it was razed to the ground.

After this, it was decided to evacuate the elephants from Moscow along with the other animals. But Shango was in such a state of excitement that it was not considered safe to lead him through the streets, and he had to be left in the Zoo. He was not left alone, however.

When they tried to take out Djindau, Shango utterly refused to part with his mate. He would not let her move from his side, not even allowing her to go near the food with which the attendants tried to entice her into the house. So they both had to stay in the Zoo.

But they were not very long together. Soon after, Djindau fell ill. She no longer bathed in the pool, no longer showered herself with sand. She stood still all day long, her head drooping sadly.

His comrade's behaviour disturbed Shango. He tried to get her to play, pushed her as if inviting her to go for a run, but Djindau never moved.

She uttered feeble cries, and when Shango would not let her alone, moved away from him. In a few days Shango realized that something was wrong with his friend and stopped worrying her.

Djindau grew worse every day. She refused the most appetizing food. And the doctor could do nothing for her.

They say that when elephants are ill they will not lie down, being afraid that, with their heavy bodies, they will not be able to get on their feet again. Whether this is so or not, the fact is that Djindau *did* stop lying down. She slept leaning against the wall, and when she moved dragged her feet with difficulty.

And yet she felt the need of air and sunlight. And one day she tried to go out, took a few steps towards the door, and suddenly collapsed heavily on to the floor and lay there.

Shango was frantic.

He rushed to Djindau and tried to help her to her feet. But Djindau could not get up. Then Shango bellowed and trumpeted, and ran into the next building. Realizing what had happened the attendants swiftly closed the door behind him. For several days Shango was kept indoors. All that time he bellowed, calling in vain for his mate. And when he was let out into the empty enclosure, it could be seen how thin he had become in those few days.

Shango did not look for Djindau. He went as usual to his favourite hill. For some time he stood motionless, and then slowly lowered his head. It drooped lower and lower, until his tusks touched the ground. Then, sinking to his knees, he drove his tusks into the soft ground as far as they would go.

He stood like this for a long time, without stirring, and as I looked at Shango I mused on the different ways in which each animal shows its grief.

Left alone, Shango grew morose and gloomy again. He would stand for hours in one place, or, stretching out his trunk, would walk past the spectators at the barrier indifferently. And not a single attendant dared to go into his enclosure, so furiously did he attack them.

MOLLY

Several years passed. The war came to an end. The Zoo once more began to fill up with animals. And a new she-elephant came to us. Her name was Molly, and she was quite tame and very docile.

She was put in a house by herself, apart from Shango.

As soon as he saw her, Shango showed signs of excitement. He refused to leave the partition behind which stood Molly, thrusting his trunk between the bars and trying unsuccessfully to reach her.

Molly was afraid of this huge stranger and would not go near him. She stood away from the partition and slowly munched the food given her. But Shango would not touch his. He kept going up to the partition and back again. Then he suddenly picked up a loaf and threw it to Molly.

Who knows what made Shango do this? Perhaps he only wanted to attract her attention. But when, looking round warily, she went to take the bread, Shango cautiously thrust his trunk through the bars and began stroking Molly with it.

After this Molly was not afraid of her neighbour any more, and a few days later they were let out into the enclosure together.

The tame and affectionate Molly had a good influence on the restless Shango. In her own way she even tried to improve his manners. When Shango rushed at the keeper, Molly moved between them and would not allow Shango to hurt the woman.

The attendants profited by this intervention and did not lock Shango up while cleaning the enclosure any more. They would call Molly, and, under her protection, sweep, clean up the enclosure, and give the elephants their food.

Shango gradually got used to the idea that he must not touch the attendants. He stopped attacking them, and nobody complained of his bad temper any more.

LITTLE MUSCOVITE

In the third year of the elephants' life together, a great event occurred in the Zoo—Molly gave birth to a baby elephant.

It was the first case of an elephant being born in captivity.

The baby was born in the night. When the attendants arrived in the morning there it stood under its mother's belly, and Shango had retreated to the farthest corner. No doubt Molly had driven him there,

for as soon as he made an attempt to come out she bellowed angrily and he hastened back again.

The elephants had to be separated, to pacify Molly. The mother and baby stayed where they were, and Shango was moved next door. And there was no difficulty about this, either. Shango himself was obviously glad to get away from the stern mamma. Hardly had they opened the gate when he slipped hastily past Molly, but not before she managed to give him a good thump with her trunk.

After Shango was removed Molly appeared much easier in her mind. She no longer watched over her baby so anxiously and even allowed the attendants to approach and touch it.

The little elephant could stand firmly on his legs almost the day after he was born. He even ventured to leave his mother's side, and kept edging up to the partition behind which was Shango.

And Shango himself took a great interest in the baby. He stretched his enormous trunk out to him between the bars and kept trying to reach him.

But Molly looked carefully after her baby, and never let him leave her side; if he moved from her ever so little she barred the way and tucked him underneath herself with her trunk.

The baby didn't quite like all this fuss. There was so much that was interesting all round, he would have liked to run about and play —and his mother made him stay beside her all the time. He would utter shrill peevish cries, stamped his feet and tried to run away.

Molly gradually allowed him to leave her side and play. It was most amusing to watch him—he would leap, shuffle, and stamp, gambolling clumsily around his mother. He was always teasing her, coiling his trunk round her feet and tail, and thrusting it cheekily into her mouth when she ate, trying to get something for himself.

When he began to run about the enclosure the baby often went up to the partition. And one day, when Molly was busy eating, the baby elephant quite unexpectedly squeezed between the bars and turned up on the other side of the partition.

Shango was charmed to see him, and began touching him with his trunk and sniffing at him. And the baby was not a bit frightened. He played with Shango, caught at his tusks, jumped at him, and the great powerful elephant shifted gently from foot to foot so as not to hurt the little one.

But how frightened Molly was when she saw her baby next to Shango! Raising her trunk she rushed up to the partition and began trumpeting loudly and anxiously.

The baby went back very reluctantly in response to her summons. Molly felt him, sniffed him all over, and at last, satisfied that he was safe and sound, drove him

under herself, probably by way of punishment. But from that day the baby elephant began going over to Shango's side more and more frequently.

Molly gradually got used to this and it was decided to open the door in the partition, so that the elephants could be together.

The baby elephant had grown a lot by that time. He could hardly stand under his mother's belly now, but was as jolly and playful as ever. And his games were becoming much more varied. He learned to manage his trunk very skilfully snatching at everything that came his way. When vegetables were brought in for the elephants, the little one would run up, pick a beetroot out of the pail with his trunk, and play ball with it, throwing it on the ground, and when it rolled away running after it and kicking at it, or he would tread on the beetroot, crush it under his foot, and slide on it as if on skates. When bran was carried in and poured into the manger the baby would get right into it and trample the bran, or would sit on it as if it were a feather mattress, and refuse to come out. And the mother stood and waited till her offspring had finished playing.

The baby elephant never got so excited over his playing as when the fodder was brought in, and he could interfere with his parents' meals.

One day, after the elephants had been given their hay, the baby lay down on it and began rolling about, even trying to turn somersaults, bending down his head, balancing on his forehead in the hay and lifting one of his hind legs. Molly stood waiting patiently for him to stop playing and let her eat.

But Shango was not so patient. He went up to the baby and tried to pull some hay from under him, and even tried to lift the naughty little thing with his trunk. But the baby simply wouldn't get up. Then

Shango coiled his trunk round the little one's tail and gave it a good tug. Up jumped the baby. And Shango tweaked his ear, gave it a shake, and led him aside. Then he went back and began calmly eating.

This chastisement apparently taught the little beggar a lesson, and after this Shango only had to go up to the manger, for the baby to stop playing at once and move out of the way.

He was a terrible little fidget, and if he could not get his parents to play, he would start teasing the woman attendant.

The moment she came into the enclosure the baby elephant would run up to her as fast as he could. The first thing he did was to stick his trunk into the pocket of her smock—she always kept a lump of sugar in there for him.

The baby elephant would take out the sugar and deposit it in his mouth. Then he would start tugging at the attendant's smock, her skirt, or her jacket, inviting her to play.

He would stretch out, first a front leg, then a hind leg for her to scratch, and sometimes he would offer his side.

One day the attendant took a new birch besom and began brushing the baby elephant with it. He liked that very much, and turned first one side, then another, and then, with an agile movement, seized the besom and ran away with it. What fun he had with it then! He whisked it over the floor so that the sawdust flew in all directions, tossed it up, caught it, tossed it up again, and brandished it, accidentally hitting Shango.

But Shango put an end to this fun immediately. He snatched the besom with his trunk, put it in his mouth, and ate it up with every sign of satisfaction. And that was the end of the game.

While the baby was still quite little he was given all sorts of names. One attendant called him Milok (Deary), another Sinok (Sonny), and a third suggested Malysh (Baby).

When the baby was a year old the time came to give him a real name. It took the people in the Zoo a long time to find the best name for the baby elephant. At last, after prolonged argument, the name Moskvich (Muscovite) was chosen. This was the most appropriate name, for he was born in the Moscow Zoo.

Moskvich is now three years old. He is quite big, almost as tall as his mother, but the whole elephant family still live together peacefully in the Zoo.

www.ingramcontent.com/pod-product-compliance
Lightning Source LLC
Chambersburg PA
CBHW022357280326
41935CB00007B/223